UNDERSTANDING ETHNIC HARMONY IN SIKKIM

ETHNIC PEACE IN SIKKIM

GAURAV SUBBA

This Book is dedicated to my blessed daughter Gaursika Cherungma Subba (Mangyoung).

Contents

Foreword — vii

Preface — ix

Acknowledgements — xi

Prologue — xiii

1. Introduction — 1

2. Major Ethnic Groups In Sikkim — 16

3. Relations Among Different Ethnic Communities: A Historical Analysis — 42

Conclusion — 69

Reference — 79

Foreword

*Gaurav Subba is from Sribadam West Sikkim. He has completed - **M.Phil.** (International Relations) (2016), Sikkim University, Sikkim. **M.A.** (International Relations/Politics) (2014), Sikkim University, Sikkim. **B.A.** (General) (2011), Sikkim Govt. College, Tadong, Gangtok East Sikkim. **B.Ed.** (Bachelor of Education) (2012), Sikkim Govt. B.Ed. College Soreng, West Sikkim. He Worked as Assistant Professor in Salesian College Siliguri, West Bengal from September 2016 – November 2016.*

His field of Specialization and research interests are: 1)An Analysis of Relationship between India, China, and Pakistan 2) History of Sikkim 3) E-Governance in Sikkim

Books published is: Global and Local Context of Good Governance: A Study in Sikkim.

Articles Published are:

1. *"Perspective of India towards Sino-Pak Collaboration" in NVEO (Natural Volatiles & Essential Oils).*
2. *"Sino-Pak Axis and It's Implications on India" in IJRAR (International Journal of Research and Analytical Reviews.*

Articles in Daily Local Newspaper of Sikkim–

1. *State and Citizens.*
2. *A Relationship of Politics with good intentions and actions.*
3. *Demonetization.*
4. *Organic Farming in Sikkim: The Trajectory of State, Farmer, Seller and Consumer.*

Etc.

Contact no: 9002687111. E-Mail: gauravsubba28@gmail.com

Preface

This Research attempts to understand the low intensity of ethnic conflict in Sikkim and some of the specific objectives are as follows:

- *To examine the mechanisms that sustains peace in Sikkim.*
- *To analyze the historical evolution of a composite Sikkim society.*

RESEARCH QUESTION

1. *What are the factors which help in the sustenance of ethnic harmony in Sikkim?*

METHODOLOGY

This research is a qualitative study which involves examination of historical events. The study adopts both primary and secondary sources. The sources are reviewed for relevant key concepts, thoughts and other facts bearing on the subject. The research consists of four chapters. The first chapter introduces the research problem, objectives of the study. The second chapter focuses Major ethnic Groups in Sikkim, discusses about the various groups in Sikkim, their histories. The third chapter tries to understand Relations among Different Ethnic Communities: A Historical analysis of major ethnic groups and their relations. The last chapter concludes with the general findings of the study.

Acknowledgements

Firstly, I would like to extend my sincere thanks to my supervisor Mr. Ph. Newton Singh for his valuable guidance, suggestions and comments which made possible to complete this research. He has dedicated his valuable time and efforts for this work.
I also like to take this opportunity to thank my teachers Dr. Manish, Dr. Teiborlang Kharsyntiew and Dr. Sebastian N. for their support, encouragement and suggestions who helped me to complete this study. I also would like to give my gratitude to all those people who has lend me supportive hands in one way or other to finish my work.
Gaurav Subba.

Prologue

To begin with history of Sikkim, the process of integration among three different tribes or ethnic groups in Sikkim we realize that there are multiple issues which can lead towards conflict, For instance in the past the whole constructive notion about dilemma of the real inhabitants of Sikkim. If we see in present day the whole idea of searching for a different identity could also be considered too. Also, if we see the issues like the demands for the reservation of seats in the state assembly by the Nepali community can give a rise to feeling of differences among the communities.

ONE

INTRODUCTION

CHAPTER I

INTRODUCTION

The word ethnicity connotes multiple definitions. Hence there is no single definition or theory of ethnicity. According to John Hutchinson and Anthony Smith (1996:4-5), the term "ethnicity" is relatively new, first appearing in the Oxford English Dictionary in 1953, but its English origins are connected to the term "ethnic," which has been in use since the middle ages. The true origins of "ethnic" have been traced back to Greece and the term ethnos, which was used in reference to band, tribe, race, a people, or a swarm (Baumann 2004).

Ethnic identity refers to an individual's ancestral heritage. Ethnocentrism is a belief that our cultural community is superior to others, resulting in hatred of any material, behavioral, or physical characteristics different than our own. Ethnicism is defined as a "movement of protest and resistance on behalf of ethnics against oppressive and exploitative outsiders." (Hutchinson and Smith (1996), as Cited in Baumann 2004). According to Hutchinson and Smith 1996:5), definition of an ethnic group,consists of six main features that Include:

1. A common *proper name*, to identify and express the "essence" of the community.

2. A myth of *common ancestry* that includes the idea of common origin in time and place and that gives an ethnie a sense of fictive kinship.

3. Shared *historical memories*, or better, shared memories of a common past or pasts, including heroes, events, and their commemoration.

4. One or more *elements of common culture*, which need not be specified but normally, include religion, customs, and language.

5. A *link* with a *homeland*, not necessarily its physical occupation by the ethnie, only its symbolic attachment to the ancestral land, as with diasporas peoples; and

6. A *sense of solidarity* on the part of at least some sections of the ethnie's population.

According to Berreman (1972, 1981) defines ethnicity as one level of social stratification or social inequality that also includes race, class, kinship, age, estate, caste, and gender. (Baumann 2004)

Berreman provides clear distinctions between ethnicity and race or class. Ethnicity is linked in a dichotic relationship with race. It is differentiated from race in that racial stratification is associated with birth-ascribed status based on physical and cultural characteristics defined by outside groups. Ethnicity is also ascribed at birth, but the ethnic group normally defines its cultural characteristics itself. Thus, racial categorizations, which are defined by the outsider, are normally laced with inaccuracies and stereotypes, while ethnic classification is normally more accurate of a cultural group because it is defined by the group itself. Yet, ethnic classifications can also be defined and used by outside groups to stereotype an ethnic community in ways that are often oversimplified and that view ethnicity as a static cultural process. Ethnicity is differentiated from class in that "social class membership and ranking is based on attributes regarded as *extrinsic* to the people who comprise the class, such as amount of income, occupation, education, consumption patterns, and 'lifestyle'" (Berreman 1981:15).

Some of the theories towards ethnicity are Primordial and Instrumental theories. Ethnicity is defined as "all those social and psychological phenomena associated with a culturally constructed group identity". Ethnic identity is defined as "that aspect of a person's self-conceptualization which results from identification with a broader group in opposition to others on the basis of perceived cultural differentiation and / or common descent." An ethnic group is classified as "any group of people who set themselves apart and/or are set by others with whom they interact or co-exist on the basis of their perceptions of cultural differentiation and/or common ancestry". (Baumann 2004).

Primordialists believe that ethnicity is a natural phenomenon with its foundations in family and kinship ties (Geertz 1963; Shils 1957); ethnicity emerges out of nepotism and reproductive fitness, narrowing down the social concept into biological terms. Isaac's basic group identity was linked to ethnic identity, which was argued to be assigned at birth and more fundamental and natural than other social links. An added component of Isaac's model is a psychological theory that addresses conflict between intertribal or ethnic groups. This latter concept is often tied to nationalist movements in modern societies. Cited in (Baumann 2004)

A major critique of the primordialist's origin of ethnicity has been that it represents a very static and naturalistic viewpoint. It does not consider culture process and other social factors that manipulate or formulate ethnic communities.

On the other hand, Instrumentalists believe that "ethnicity is socially constructed, and people have the ability to cut and mix from a variety of ethnic heritages and cultures to form their own individual or group identities" (Hutchinson and Smith 1996:9). Instrumentalists' theory has been characterized as concerned "with the role of ethnicity in the mediation of social relations and the negotiation of access to resources, primarily economic and political resources" (Jones 1997:72). Jones (1974:75) argues that instrumentalists fall into two categories: "those who focus on the socio-structural and cultural dimensions of ethnicity and adopt a more objectivist approach; and those who focus on the interpersonal relationship and behavioral aspects of ethnicity and take a more subjectivist stance" Cited in (Baumann 2004).

According to Baumann (2004) Barth viewed ethnic identity as an "individualistic strategy" in which individuals move from one identity to another to "advance their personal economic and political interests, or to minimize their losses" (Jones 1997:74). Following Barth, ethnic identity forms through boundary maintenance and interaction between individuals (Baumann 2004).

Depending on each social interaction, a person's ethnic identity can be perceived or presented in various ways. Overall, interaction between individuals does not lead to an assimilation or homogenization of culture. Instead, cultural diversity and ethnic identity are still maintained, but in a no static form. Cultural traits and even individuals can cross over ethnic boundaries, which in turn can transform an ethnic group over time.

In contrast to Barth, Cohen (1974) "placed [a] greater emphasis on the ethnic group as a *collectively* organized strategy for the protection of economic and political interests" (Jones 1997:74). Ethnic groups share common interests, and in pursuit of these interests they develop "basic organizational functions: distinctiveness or boundaries; communication; authority structure; decision making procedure; ideology; and socialization" (Cohen 1974: xvi–xvii). Overall, Jones (1997:74) suggests that both Barth and Cohen "focus on the organizational features of ethnicity, and ethnicity is regarded as constituting the shared beliefs and practices that provide a group with the boundary maintenance and organizational dimensions necessary to maintain, and compete for, socioeconomic resources." [1]

Jones suggests that a true understanding of ethnicity can be viewed through "practice theory", which attempts to address "the relationship between objective conditions and subjective perceptions." Jone's definition of practice theory is grounded in Bourdieu's (1977) theory of practice in which he developed the concept of habitus (Baumann 2004). Following Bourdieu, Jones states that "the habitus is made up of durable dispositions towards certain perceptions and practices (such as those relating to sexual division of labour, morality, tastes, and etc.), which become part of an individual's sense of self at an early age, and which can be transposed from one context to another." Under practice theory, ethnicity is not static reflection of culture, nor is it produced entirely by social interaction and boundary maintenance.

Rather, "the intersubjective construction of ethnic identity is grounded in the shared subliminal dispositions of the habitus, which shape, and are shaped by, objective commonalities of practice shared habitus engender feelings of identification among people similarly endowed". The habitus is multidimensional and can differ in various social situations. Ethnicity is understood or seen as being in a constant state of change and reproduction within these different social contexts. Individuals are viewed as "social agents acting strategically in the pursuit of interests." Collectively, ethnicity is viewed as a "shared disposition of habitus"[2] Cited in (Baumann 2004).

Since this paper deals with the notion of ethnic peace or why there is less intensity of conflict in Sikkim. So, as to preserve communal harmony. Thus, we need to understand the arguments/ideas on ethnic conflict.

Most states are composed of more than one ethnic group. Sometimes these groups are not accepted as full members of this state or the nation. Number of ethnic groups demands more rights and recognition which can lead in many cases to ethnic conflicts.

To understand ethnic conflict to some extent we can see that ethnic conflicts within a state belong to the identity conflicts that are a type of internal conflicts. Apart from, identity conflicts there are other types of internal conflicts, governance conflicts, racial conflicts, and environmental conflicts.

Sometimes the term "ethnic conflict" is used to describe a wide range of internal conflicts. The dominant aspect of identity conflicts is ethnic, religious, tribal, or linguistic differences. These conflicts often involve a mixture of identity and the search for security where the prime contention concerns the devolution of power. This was the main type of war in Srilanka, Palestine in the 1980s. identity conflicts are sub-divided into territorial, ethnic or minority conflicts and assertions of religious and struggle for self-determination.

Ethnic conflicts can be defined as conflicts between ethnic groups within a multi-ethnic state. According to Michael E. Brown, an ethnic conflict is a dispute about important political, economic, cultural, or territorial issues between two or more ethnic communities (Ismayilov, Gursel G. "Ethnic Conflicts and Their Causes." 17).

Many, ethnic conflicts result in a significant loss of life, a serious denial of basic human rights and considerable material destruction, some escalating into interethnic or internal war.

The desire for secession or independence from an existing state, the demand for greater autonomy within a state, or recognition and protection of minority interest within a society are three general issues of ethnic conflicts. (Ismayilov n.d.)

As we look in the age of globalization where we find different people across the globe have come closer through improved means of communication and technology, where different cultures too have started sharing a common space. This has indeed turned the world into a "global village". Therefore, there seems to be a gradual emergence of consensus on the popular acceptance of the worldview that democracy essays. However, democracy talks about the majoritarian choice and what constitutes the majoritarian choice is determined by the majoritarian culture. This has a deep impact on the relations regarding those culture labeled as "minority". The majoritarian culture, also called as the popular culture, casts a shadow of dominance over minority cultures through processes of subjugation and homogenization. This has been one of the major challenges among states and regions endowed with plurality of ethnos and cultures.

The word "minority" is derived from the Latin word minor, meaning "smaller" or "fewer". It can refer to a purely quantitative or statistical relationship. The term "minority" was proposed in 1932 by Donald Young as a way of transcending the hereditarian implication of the word "race," which at that time was in a popular as well as scientific use to refer to what is called as "ethnic groups" today.

Multiculturalism is not the first paradigm to discuss about the issue of social and ethnic equations. Prior to multiculturalism gaining currency, there were mainly three models that explained the social interaction.

First, Assimilation, which talks of mingling of the minority social, groups into the dominant majority social groups. Here the social process refers to the subordinate group being subjugated by the dominant ones through the adoption of the dominant cultures.

Second, Integration, the two social groups come together to form a separate force taking some aspect of the former and some of the latter.

Third is Segregation, where the different groups of the society can progress through separate allocation of space, which has been best exemplified through the policy of Apartheid in South Africa.

However, today, Multiculturalism has become one of the most discussed and debated paradigm on the issue of ethnic and social equations, due to the characteristics of the world which has become increasingly multiple and diverse in the social, familial, and communal relations. Moreover, multiculturalism asserts the rights of the minority through this framework as pointed out by political theorist like Will Kymlicka.

Multiculturalism by recognizing the differences among the cultural groups seeks to protect the rights of the cultural minority groups and address the issue of their exclusion or dilution from the larger cultural space. This provides recognition of their allegiance to the state without expecting them to be exactly same as the others. Although this may raise several problems, theoretical and practical, the policy of affirmative action has helped in protecting the rights of the minorities.

The policy of multiculturalism not only addresses the issue of diversity among the people, but also protects the rights of the minorities thereby ensuring the ethos of human rights and give the minorities a space to assert their identities without any tension among ethnic communities in the country.

Policy of multiculturalism can be seen as a viable pragmatic approach to address the issue of conflicts among the different ethnic groups. Internal conflicts in the state is often result of the perceived notions or ideas formed by a community against another community on the basis of certain attitude and perceptions driven by biased prejudices and contempt. This provides the necessary ingredients of conflict among the various ethnic groups. Therefore, there is a need for a discourse shaped by the ideals of multiculturalism to inculcate a multicultural attitude to promote the idea of diversity of cultures irrespective of whether they are dominant or minority community.

The need for multiculturalism emerges out of a concern for having a peaceful co-existence among communities sharing a politico-cultural space (Vaiphei 2008).

As we know that since there are three major ethnic/linguistic groups in Sikkim which again we find there are various sub-groups. Also, if we investigate the influx of various population and their rising demands such as for the acceptance of COI (certificate of identification), this may be one of the causes to give a rise to conflict situation in future.

Thus, to prevent such things from happening we can consider the Canadian model of multiculturalism which may give insight to deal with issues related with contestation of space in assertion of identity and cultures; and much to think of what will constitute as the right response in addressing the ethnic equations so that a situation of peace can be sustained through the dialogues among the different ethnic groups. (Vaiphei 2008)

Since, Ethnicity is a complex phenomenon that refers to the sense of peoplehood or the feeling shared by the members of the group. An ethnic group has its own sub-structure and sub-culture parallel to the larger society (punekar 1974: 3). The affective dimension of ethnic identity is also emphasized by cohen (1974) in the African context. Firstly, ethnicity is understood through the caste/religion/culture/language background in particular cases of a single group.

Secondly, in larger context, it is defined as comprising of more than one and many groups based on privilege realization reserved for that combined/composite group which has been the imposed identity. Ethnicity affects the life of the individuals and groups in many ways. Indeed, ethnicity has become a 'resource' an affiliation to which ultimately involves the realization of 'privilege' for a section of the society. Role played by the constitutional provisions strengthens the ethnic identity. Ethnic groups have over time become strong 'interest' group and ethnicity a 'resource'. This dimension has created conflict situations (Lama 1994).

Ethnic conflicts are basically conflicting of interest group (for example, African studies of Epstein 1978; charsley 1974; cohen 1974). Which identity will be stressed in a given situation depends on the situation itself (caplan, 1981) these conflicts in turn heighten the ethnic identities (punekar 1986:112).

Indeed, the society in Sikkim may be conceived as 'ethnically diverse' and in poly-ethnic society like Sikkim, political and economic interests in terms of privileges shapes ethnic inter-group relations. So, the ethnicity in Sikkim may be envisaged between 'them' and us for the purpose of identification. This has been according to wallman's definition of ethnicity in which he says that "...ethnicity is the process by which 'their' differences are used to enhance the sense of 'us' for purpose of organization or identification" (wallman 1979: 3).

In the light of above definition, the ethnicity of the ethnicity in Sikkim may be revealed by discussing the three following perspectives.

1. Ethnicity based on tribal identity
2. Ethnicity based on combined tribal identity vis-à-vis non-tribal identity.
3. Ethnicity based on socio-political identity-a large, combined identity of various ethnic groups.[3]

Until 1975, a hereditary monarchy, Sikkim became the youngest member of the Indian union, since it entered the mainstream of national life after a violent popular revolutionary upsurge. The political metamorphosis by which this 22nd state was added to the Indian Union was an event of not merely local significance but one which had international importance. This merger has inaugurated a new age and a new political system for the people of Sikkim. The Governor as the Chief Executive assumed the office and the first elected Chief Minister of Sikkim was appointed. The Government machinery being thus set up by the Constitution India, Sikkim started traversing the path of democracy.

There is now a council of ministers headed by the chief ministers who are held responsible for their actions to the legislative assembly of a total of 32 members. This legislative assembly is the only law-making body in the state. As the constitution of India envisages the establishment of a High Court in each state there is one as the Apex court for civil and criminal cases. The state has a Secretariat which is divided into various departments and different sections. The CM is the political head, and the Secretary is the administrative head of the department. The Chief Secretary is at the apex of the administrative hierarchy who heads the hierarchical organizations of the Secretariat.

Sikkim is divided into four districts and nine sub-divisions to facilitate local administration. There is a district officer called district magistrate as the head of the district administration under whom there are sub-divisional and block level officers to discharge administrative functions. For the effective administration of villages, a two tier Panchayati Raj System has been established in the state. The gram panchayat and the Zilla panchayat play an active role in the developmental works.[4]

It is not much known about the early people settled down as the main native habitants in the land of Sikkim before it came to be acknowledged that the Lepchas were the autochthones prior to the migration of Bhutias from Tibet in the 15th or 16th century. Although the opinions differ regarding the origin of the Sikkim's first inhabitants, it is now generally believed that the Lepchas were here in this land to accommodate the influx of the Bhutia immigrants sometimes in the 15th century. The other immigrants to find a niche here were the Nepalese. Sikkim is found to be a safe haven for all these people to live together in harmony without discord. These three communities are considered the main and distinct people of Sikkim. (Gurung 2011)

To begin with history of Sikkim, the process of integration among three different tribes or ethnic groups in Sikkim we realize that there are multiple issues which can lead towards conflict, For instance in the past the whole constructive notion about dilemma of the real inhabitants of Sikkim. If we see in present day the whole idea of searching for a different identity could also be considered too. Also, if we see the issues like the demands for the reservation of seats in the state assembly by the Nepali community can give a rise to feeling of differences among the communities.

But as we can realize ourselves that there are multiple ethnic-religious groups in Sikkim who have their own interests irrespective of the groups and try to maintain their identity. Which leads us to the idea of **"us** versus **them"** and many things which can give rise to ethnic conflict, but still, we find there is sustenance of peace or there is no violence in a physical manner and ethnic groups of Sikkim lives in harmony, this in a way Sikkim as a multi-ethnic state can be a good model for ensuring peace.

OBJECTIVES

The Research attempts to understand the low intensity of ethnic conflict in Sikkim and some of the specific objectives are as follows:

- To examine the mechanisms that sustains peace in Sikkim.
- To analyze the historical evolution of a composite Sikkim society.

RESEARCH QUESTION

1. What are the factors which help in the sustenance of ethnic harmony in Sikkim?

METHODOLOGY

This research is a qualitative study which involves examination of historical events. The study adopts both primary and secondary sources. The sources are reviewed for relevant key concepts, thoughts and other facts bearing on the subject. The research consists of four chapters. The first chapter introduces the research problem, objectives of the study. The second chapter focuses Major ethnic Groups in Sikkim, discusses about the various groups in Sikkim, their histories. The third chapter tries to understand Relations among Different Ethnic Communities: A Historical analysis of major ethnic groups and their relations. The last chapter concludes with the general findings of the study.

[1] Baumann, Timothy. "Defining Ethnicity." *The SAA Archaeological record.*, 2004: 3.

[2] Baumann, Timothy. "Defining Ethnicity." *The SAA Archaeological record.*, 2004: 3.

[3] Lama, Mahendra P, ed. *SIKKIM Society Polity Economy Environment*. New Delhi: Indus Publishing Company, 1994.

[4] Dewan, Dr. Dick B. *Education in Sikkim An Historical Retrospect Pre-Merger and Post-Merger Period*. Tender Buds Academy, July 2012.

TWO

MAJOR ETHNIC GROUPS IN SIKKIM

CHAPTER II
Major Ethnic Groups in Sikkim

Sikkim, a small Himalayan state of the Indian union, is a multi-cultural society cohabited by a multiple cultural-linguistic group of which the Lepchas (also called Rongs/ Monpas), the Bhutias (also called Denzongpas/Lhopas) and the Nepalis (also called Gorkhas/Paharias) form major communities in Sikkim. Lamaist Buddhism and Hinduism are the two major religions and apart from it, we find Christianity also. Besides, a small group of the population still practices animism, found particularly among the Lepchas and mongoloid stocks of the Nepalis (Gurung 2011).

Other than the major ethnic groups of present-day Sikkim—the Lepchas, the Bhutias, and the Nepalis, the communities like Sherpas, Yolmos/Kagatey, Limboos (Tsong) etc. are also important in any analysis of ethnicity and identity formation mainly in view of what the communities think and what others say about them. Certain other Nepali tribes/castes like Mangars, Tamangs (Murmi), Gurungs, Rais etc. also deserve special mention in view of the ethno-political scenario of Sikkim. Over the decade's social mobility among the three ethnic communities has increased along with the events of inter-community marriages and social interaction though distinct identity of each community is maintained.

The history of Sikkim exists in varying narratives. One of the narratives suggests that the Tibetan lamas burned the documents when they first encountered the 'Monpas' or the inhabitants of the lower Himalaya. This in a way resulted in the disappearance of recorded documentary evidence. There also is a strong presence of oral narrative. Most of the histories of these communities are found in the folklores and in the forms of oral traditions.

The chapter discusses the major ethnic communities in Sikkim and their histories. As mentioned above, there are three major communities in Sikkim—Lepcha, Bhutia and Nepalese. Within the Nepalese, there are multiple groups having different customs, dialects, and traditions. Among the three major communities, it is believed that the Lepchas are the first inhabitants. However, there are also anthropologists who believe that there were three different tribes inhabiting Sikkim before the advent of the Lepchas in Sikkim.

H. Siiger writes, "*...there are ancient traits of various kinds contributing to the suggestion that the Lepchas originally came from the East. On entering Sikkim the Lepchas found three tribes already in possession of the country, viz. the Na-ang or Na-ong, the Chang, and the Mon, of which the Na-ong were the earliest inhabitants. Risley too acknowledges the existence of the* *tribe called Na-ong, and associates the tribe with the popular feat of building a legendary tower (Babel) at Daramdin in west Sikkim. He considers the tribe extinct. The new encyclopedia Britannica also mentions "the Lepchas were early inhabitants of the region, apparently assimilating the Naong, Chang, Mon, and other tribes."*

The tribes in question may be the product of misrepresentation of the source but Mainwaring considers "Na-ong" as one of the sections of the Lepchas. He further writes that other two tribes, i.e., Chang and Mon, as mentioned by Siiger, are most probably the "Tsong", by which name Limboos in Sikkim were/ are known, and "Mon" should have meant the Lepchas (Gurung; 2011).

The Bhutias and the Lepchas have lived together for centuries under a common Bhutia-Lepcha's identity. However, there emerged a trend wherein the Lepchas, through various activities and propaganda, emphasize on the maintenance of a separate Lepcha identity. Similarly, Limboos also do not identify themselves with the larger Nepalis identity. Similarly, different sub-cultural groups within the larger Nepali community also speak in terms of respective group identity.

There are associations/organizations of almost all these small communities through which they articulate respective group interest and group identity. Thus, it is necessary that these identities of different communities, including the small communities, should be studied. But it is also important to find out, what is the force behind maintenance of ethnic harmony in a multiethnic state like Sikkim.

These three ethnic groups—the Lepchas, the Bhutias and the Nepalis settled in the state at different times. The Lepchas and a few Kirati people are considered the original inhabitants of the Sikkim. On the other hand, the Bhutias and Nepalis are immigrants. The Bhutia and Lepchas mostly follow Buddhism while the Nepalese mostly follow Hinduism. The following section discusses in detail the various ethnic communities in Sikkim.

The Lepchas

Lepchas, meaning 'Ravine Folk', the earliest Lepcha settlers were believers in the Bon faith or Mune faith based on spirits, good and bad, witchcrafty and exorcism were very common. The well-known deities of the Lepcha are It Bumoo, Rom, Itbu Debu Rom, Kongchen, Konglo and Tamsang Thing. Major festivals of the Lepcha is the Namsoong marking the beginning of the New Year. The Lepcha priests are known as Bomthing. Lepchas population is concentrated in the central part of Sikkim areas encompassing the confluence of Lachen and Lachung rivers and Dickchu. They settle on steep hillsides living on agriculture of paddy, cardamom, and oranges. Life in a Lepcha dwelling is very simple, male wears a dress called Pagi, and the female wears 2(two) pieces dress called Tago and Domdyan. They speak Lepcha and are good at archery used for hunting and gatherings of food. The polyandry marriages are permitted amongst the Lepchas although this is now becoming very rare. The Nuptial customs are quite intriguing. After, both the parties have evinced interest in establishing marital relations, the boys' maternal uncle approaches the parents of the girl with some bottles of liquor, scarf, and some money. When the marriage ends, the husband must pay some money to the girl's parents. The government feels protective towards the Lepchas, believing that they represent a conservative force, a balance wheel which helps save a way of life from being overwhelmed by western culture. (Diyali n.d., p.7). It is claimed that the

Lepchas call themselves 'Rong', the people living in ravines, migrated to the present site from Assam hills, are the earliest settlers of land. They have elaborate terms for rivers, water lives, flora, and fauna of Sikkim unlike any community found in the country. However, their current name itself is a gift of the Nepali language, "Lapcho", the residents of the heap of stone, or the stone house. It is claimed that the Rongs were organized by Turve Panu (king), their king or chief, in the hoary past after some generations, kingship came to an end and the tribe switched off to a system of chieftainship. It is said that Thekong-tek, the Lepcha chief, was instrumental in installing the Bhutia rule in Sikkim by associating himself with the Tibetan migrants. Accordingly, a dozen of Lepcha chiefs was accorded with the status of Dzongpens, or regional rulers or the governors, by the first Bhutia theocrat, Phuntso Namgyal (1642-1670). These Dzongpens along with another dozen of Bhutia councilors came to be known as the Kazis, the Sikkimese aristocrats, in course of time (Sinha, A C 1975). These two dozen Kazis inter-married among themselves and many of the Lepchas became Buddhist. However, the Lepcha Kazis came to be known as the 'created or the fashioned' ones against the Bhutia 'the flowing from on high'; the lower and the higher order respectively of the Kazis. Ethnological literature on the Lepchas suggests that it is a community of 'mild, timid, and peaceful persons who are devoid of all sorts of conflict'. It is said that there is no word for violence and conflict in their language. By tradition, they are inhabitants of inner Himalayan highland and they lived in Zongu Lepcha reserve, a preserve of the former royal family.

The Bhutias

The Bhutias, the other community, are evenly distributed throughout the state of Sikkim, where they are the major inhabitants, they are known as the Lachungpas and Lachenpas. They name their own traditional legal system as *Dzumsa* (public meeting place) to settle their disputes. The Bhutia aristocrats are known as Kazis. They speak Sikkimese language, which in fact, is a dialect of Tibetan language and the script is the same. Marriage in a Bhutia family is arranged through negotiations by the paternal or maternal uncle of the boy who goes to the brides' place with gifts to ask for the hand to tie a knot with his nephew. The traditional dress of the female member is known as Bakhu, Honju, and Pangdin. (It is a symbol of married women).

The word Bhutia is derived from the name of the place "Bhot", i.e., Tibet, to which the Bhutias of Sikkim originally belonged. The migration of the Bhutias into Sikkim probably begun during the fifteenth and sixteenth century. Maharaja Thutop Namgyal and Maharani Yeshey Dolma Namgyal have also subscribed to this viewpoint and added further that the migration took place continuously in many ways and through different routes, from the northern and western passes of Sikkim. According to a popular version, the religious strife between the Yellow-Hat-Sect (Gelukpas) and the Red-Hat-Sect (Nyngmapas) in Tibet forced many followers of Red-Hat-Sect to flee Tibet along with the leader Khye Bhumsa after their defeat. They settled in the Chumbi valley, an inalienable part of Sikkim then. Initially the nature loving, and friendly Lepchas did not object but as the migration continued, the Lepchas Athing, Thekong Tek, advised the Panu Hyum to take stock of the situation. It is said that the Lepcha Panu (king) was treacherously murdered. According to the folklore/legend, Khye Bhumsa later sought hospitable relationship with the Lepcha spiritual leader (Athing) Thekong Tek which was then solemnized by a 'blood-brotherhood' pact at Kabi and solicited blessing for son. Having realized their bleak future in Tibet, they made Chumbi valley their permanent settlement and gradually spread to other parts of Sikkim (Gurung; 2011).

These early settlers from Tibet presently are known as Denzongpa or Lhori while those who have migrated to Sikkim during the eighteenth and nineteenth centuries were called Khampa or Pu-pa and considered different from the Denzongpa or the Lhori. Those who have migrated in the twentieth century, especially after Chinese occupation of Tibet, are referred to as Tibetans. The distinctions, however, has been narrowed down due to the use of all embracing generic term "Bhutia" in the Scheduled Tribes Order of 1978 (Gurung; 2011).

Following the classification given by Risley, the Bhutias of Sikkim may be grouped under three categories. Firstly, the six families descended directly from Khye-Bhumsa. They are Yul Thenpa, Lingzerpa, Zhantarpa or Sangdarpa, Tshegyu Tarpa, Nyungyepa and Tshepa. The last four families (clans) are also called Tungdu-Rusi or 'the four families of a 1,000 collections' (Gurung; 2011).

The second category includes those who migrated after the exodus of Khye Bhumsa. They are called Khampas or Bebtsen Gye by virtue of having founded eight families namely Gansapa, Namchangpgopa, Chungiopa, Ethenpa, Phenchungpa, Phempunadik, Namnakpa, and Nachingpa. The third category is comprised of those who migrated at various time since the establishment of the Bhutia rule in Sikkim. They are called Rui-Chhung or the little families with eight important branches, the Chumbipa (immigrants from Kham in Tibet and Ha in Bhutan and settled near Chumbi valley). And Lopen Lhundup (migrated from Ha and Paro in Bhutan and settled in Lachen and Lachung valleys). Each of these families or clans is further subdivided into several subfamilies (Gurung; 2011).

The Sikkimese Bhutia language was a spoken dialect and for all literary, cultural, and educational pursuits, Tibetan was used in the past. It was also the official language of Sikkim before the merger. All government gazette notifications were brought out in Tibetan language, including the official newsletter 'Sikkim Herald'. After 1975 efforts have been made to develop Sikkimese Bhutia as a distinct language in Sikkim, and in 1977 the status of official language has been accorded to it.

The social-cultural organizations of the Bhutias like Bhutia Kay-Rab-Yargay Tsogpo, is dedicated in conserving and developing the culture, tradition, religion, language, and literature of Bhutias of Sikkim. It was established in 1983. It has conducted many seminars, workshops, and meetings with the objective of contributing towards the promotion of the Bhutia and their rich culture. The organization also helps publication of books and dictionaries besides encouraging people who are engaged in the promotion of the Bhutia culture, art, literature, and language by felicitating them. Almost all the Bhutias of Sikkim are bilingual/trilingual and speak Bhutia language as well as Nepalis and Lepcha languages fluently. The language is taught up to the under-graduate level. The majority of the Sikkimese Bhutias are the followers of Lamaist Buddhism but sympathizer of Christianity is also rising in recent past.

Bodhisattva is their chief deity followed by the guardian deity, including local deities, family deities, village deities and mount Kanchendzonga. Monastery or Gumpa is their place of worship and the Bhutia lama (spiritual leader) performs all customary rituals. Their main concentration is in the North-District, especially in Lachen and Lachung villages but, of late, they are numerically the largest among the tribes of Sikkim in the east district, especially in Gangtok.

In 1840 the Bhutias were approximately 1995 out of a total of 7000 populations. In 1873 they were 1500 persons out of a total of 5000 populations. In 1891 the figure shot up to 4,894 persons among whom 1,966 were males, 1,960 females and 968 were children. The Bhutias were mostly the traders and herdsmen earlier but a sizable number were also engaged in cultivation. They generally preferred hilly terrain, high altitude, and cold climate for habitation. With the consolidation of political power and establishment of religious hegemony after 1642 not only the settlement pattern was changed but the social stratification too began to take shape in the form of Royal family, Lamas, Kazis and the commoners (Gurung; 2011).

The lamas (spiritual leader), who often belonged to the noble families of Tibet were the custodian of the important monasteries of Sikkim like Dubdi, Pemiongchi, Tashiding etc., besides exercising significant influence, as advisers to the Chogyal, in the political-administrative affairs of the state. The monasteries were in possession of huge, landed property over which the lamas enjoyed both revenue and administrative control. The Kazis, on the other, were landlords or Zamindars, mostly belonging to the Bhutia-Lepchas groups, who enjoyed immense economic and political power in a feudal bureaucratic and economic setup under the Chogyal. Within their territorial jurisdiction they also exercised power of adjudication. The involvement of British in Sikkim's affair (more explicitly after 1861) saw a reduction in the political and economic powers of the Kazis and Lamas, on the one hand, and settlement of certain Nepalese businessmen and peasants and economic prosperity of the protected state of Sikkim on the other (Gurung; 2011).

The economic prosperity led to competition over resources and growth of resentment against the policies of the British political officer in general and Nepalese in particular. The resentment, however, led to introduction of certain legislative measures in favor of the Bhutias and Lepchas in the form of prohibition of transaction of the Bhutia-Lepchas land to the Nepalese and other communities (Revenue Order No. 1, 1897/1917), differential rate of revenue between the Bhutia-Lepchas and the Nepalese peasants (1915) and settlement laws.

In the wake of the demands for abolition of Zamindari system followed by peasant's movement of 1949-50, certain economic changes were introduced such as abolition of Zamindari system (excluding 15 private estates of the Chogyal and 5 monastery estates) and payment of revenue directly to the state. Though the effect of the economic reform on the land share pattern was marginal (due to continuation of the Revenue Order No. 1 and absence of ceiling and tenancy reforms), but their sources of income had been drastically reduced. They, however, were apprehensive of the government notification no. 3082/L.R., 1954 which had the intention to detect the excess land over the upper ceiling of 20 acres and distribution of the same among the landless masses (Gurung; 2011).

They desired for protecting their hereditary right over land and since they exercised influence at the decision-making level, the successive land reform measures to a large extent have remained ineffective.

In 1978, the Bhutia community has been recognized as one of the Scheduled Tribes of Sikkim. The 1978 order included eight other Bhutias namely Tromopa, Dopthapa, Sherpa, Yolmo, Kagatey, Drukpa, Tibetans and Chumbipa within the definition of the term Bhutia. Though these groups have been recognized as Bhutias, they are not benefitted by the Revenue Order No 1 which prohibits sale or purchase of Bhutia-Lepchas land by other communities, including the Nepalese. However, they can contest elections from the 12 Bhutia-Lepchas seats reserved in the Legislative Assembly of Sikkim (Gurung; 2011).

Traditionally, Bhutias are assertive and industrious people. The young generation Bhutias are well educated, well informed and are conscious of their rights and privileges both as a Sikkimese and as a citizen of a democratic country.

Their access to best available educational institutions in the country and abroad together with the facilities extended to the scheduled tribes' community, the Bhutias are overwhelmingly represented in the top-level bureaucratic posts and in other decision-making institutions. Their representation in such institutions often benefited the community immensely in terms of employment and other economic opportunities as compared to other communities of Sikkim. Being the ruling community, the Bhutias did not have a political organization of their own before 1947 as their interests were adequately protected and represented through various proclamations issued by the Chogyal from time to time. However, some pressure groups of the traditional landlords and lamas of monasteries were present from the very early days in Sikkim. Being parties to the ruling clique, these groups played important roles both in creating channels for articulating their demands and influencing political decision in favor of the group.

The non-associational group of the landlords was very powerful and enjoyed both administrative and judicial authorities within their territorial jurisdiction. The officials of the Darbar were mostly chosen from among the Kazis and by virtue of their proximity with the Chogyal, they used to influence decisions in their favor. It is said that the Kazis were instrumental in denying the status of "hereditary subjects" of Sikkim to the Limboos even when one seat was reserved for them in 1967". In 1978, out of 13 Bhutia-Lepcha's candidates who were taken in the IAS cadre selection 10 belonged to the Kazi group. Similarly, the Bhutia spiritual leaders, called lamas, also used to form a formidable pressure group in Sikkim. Their activities extended from advising the ruler in political affairs of the country to management of monasteries, including the monetary allocation for monasteries and selection of religious performance out of the state treasury. The custom was that the Chogyal could not avoid the advice tendered by the Lhade Mede, the council of incarnate Lamas (Gurung; 2011).

Their influence in the political affairs of the state was such that in March 1958 one seat was reserved for the monasteries in the state council as Sangha seat. It was politically very active during the 1970s as the members of the organization were apprehensive of the fate of the Chogyal and the status of Sikkim as a Buddhist state after its merger with a democratic secular India. They were instrumental in maintaining the socio-cultural and political identity of Sikkim even after the merger.

The political organization of the Bhutias, called Sikkim Nationalist Party, was formed in 1948 with an objective to oppose the demands of the Sikkim State Congress for accession with India, establishment of responsible government and abolition of the Zamindari system. It was communal in its propaganda and feudal in its outlook, and as such, failed to function as a political party. Sengupta writes, "the Sikkim National Party has sprung up with a curious programme which may be called the very anti-thesis of the policy of Sikkim State Congress". For the Sikkim National Party, also called Chogyal's party, the Lepchas and Bhutias alone were indigenous Sikkimese whereas Nepalese were considered immigrants from Nepal. The political and other social organizations that are formed after the merger in 1975 differ from their earlier counterparts in terms of composition and the group to which they appeal for support.

Genuinely, they cannot be considered ethnic organizations of the Bhutias but are tribal organizations dominantly led by the Bhutias. The Denzong People's Congress (DPC), a registered political party, the Denzong Tribal Yargay Chogpa (DTYC), Sikkim Tribal Welfare Associations (STWA), the Denzong Lhaday Yangki Chakchen (association of Buddhist monk of Sikkim), the Bhutia Kay-Rab-Yargay Tsogpo (BKRYT) are such organizations to name a few. The Bhutia Kay-Rab-Yargay Tsogpo is a social organization dedicated in conserving and developing the culture, tradition, religion, language, and literature of Bhutias of Sikkim. It was established in 1983. It conducts seminars, workshops, and meetings with the objective of contributing towards the promotion of the Bhutia language and their rich culture (Gurung; 2011).

The association of Buddhist monks of Sikkim and 'Concerned Citizens of Sikkim' became popular during 1994 in respect to the protest movement unleashed against the construction of Rathang Chu Hydel Project on religious-environmental grounds. The project was abandoned in 1997. Thus, religion has been an important factor and strength which binds the tribals together but inspite of several unifications at the ethnic level, it is yet to be accomplished mainly due to existence of separate organizations of the tribal communities with distinct ideological beliefs and propaganda. The Bhutia way of life, which is generally highlighted as Sikkimese identity, is something that irks other tribal groups (Gurung; 2011).

The Nepalis

The Nepali community constitutes 70% of the total population of Sikkim. A major sub-cultural stock of the Nepalese is the Kiratis. Other communities of Nepalese are Pradhan or Newars; service castes are Kamis, Damais and Sarkis; priests or pundit are Sharmas; warriors' classes are Basnets, Thakuris and Chettris. The language spoken by Nepalese is of Devanagri script. Understood and spoken commonly all over the state, which has got its inclusion in the 8th Schedule of the Indian constitution. In terms of religious beliefs, the population of Sikkim is predominantly Hindu (68%) Buddhist is quite a large community (27%) and Christian represents 3% of the total population.

Nepalese constitute ethno-linguistically the majority group in Sikkim. But before going into the details of the subject there are certain ambiguities associated with the word 'Nepalis' which required clarification in the first place. Firstly, who is a Nepalis? Is he a citizen of Nepal or a member of an ethnic group or a caste or one who speaks Nepali language? To an average Sikkimese or for an Indians as such, Nepali means those who have migrated from Nepal and speak the language which is identified as Nepali/ Khaskura or Gorkha and belonging to Aryan languages group as distinct from Tibeto-Burman languages or dialects like Bhutia, Tibetan, Lepcha, and Limboos etc.

Over the past decades there have been attempts to undermine the history of the existence of various groups who are now known to the outsiders as Nepalese. The Sikkimese Nepalese belong to Sikkim in the same way as the Bhutias and the Lepchas do.

Secondly, Nepali is not a complete homogeneous group like that of the Lepchas. It is a conglomeration of different and distinct tribes and communities which can be broadly classified under two basic groups: Mongoloids and Aryans. Thirdly, there is a lack of cohesion between "those who are considered as Nepalese" and "those who consider themselves as Nepalese". For example, the Limboos in Sikkim are called Nepalese but they themselves do not consider so. Similarly, Sherpas or Yolmos are subsumed constitutionally as a Bhutia group but they acknowledge themselves as Nepalese. Fourthly, an identity of a Nepali cannot be established only because he speaks Nepali language. A Bhutia or Lepchas or Marwari may not know any language other than Nepali, yet he is never considered as Nepali but a Limboo or Rai or Gurung may speak no Nepali but his own language or dialect, yet he is Nepali to the outside world. So, Nepali identity is not just linguistic, but also racial and above all historical.

Nepali is just an umbrella term under which various tribes and communities find a homogenous representation. The following groups are generally included as Nepali such as Bahun (Brahmin), Thakuri, Chhetri, Newar, Rai, Gurung, Tamang, Limboo, Mangar, Jogi, Bhujel, Thami, Yolmo, Sherpa, Dewan, Mukhia, Sunar, Sarki, Kami and Damai. Except those who belonged to Aryan stock and basically Hindus by religion like Bahun, Chhetri, Thakuri, Kami,

Sarki, and Damai who represent north Indian physical features, rest of the Nepali sub-cultural groups have their own languages or dialects, traditions, cultures, heroes and habits, religion and belong to Mongoloid racial stock. If taken together, they consist of roughly about 50 percent of Sikkim's total population the Bahun, Chhetri etc. speak Nepali language which belongs to Indo-Aryan group of languages with Nagri script like Hindi while the Mongoloids stocks are mostly bi-lingual, i.e., speak their own language/dialect other than Nepali language. Nepalese, therefore, is a mixture of Aryan and Mongoloid racial groups (Gurung; 2011).

In the history of the settlement of different ethnic groups in Sikkim the Nepalese seemed to have followed a natural process due to the prevalence of free intercourse between the people of Nepal and Sikkim, the territorial contiguity existing between the two neighbors, porous and flexible borders and, of course, war. From many eminent social investigators and anthropologists like Subba, Mackean, Risley, Hooker, Sinha etc. it is safely established that some of the Nepali tribes or communities belonging to Mongoloid (Matwali) groups like the Limboos (Tsongs), the Mangars, the Gurungs, the Tamangs, the Rais etc. either lived in Sikkim or in places contiguous to it even before the arrival of the Lepchas or were contemporaries of the latter. R.K. Sprigg writes, "the Limboos were living in Sikkim before there was Sikkim for them to live in". Mangers, now a constituent of the larger Nepali community, are among the early inhabitants of Sikkim, and are often referred to as contemporary of the Lepchas. According to J.D. Hooker, Mangars were the aborigines of Sikkim, but were driven by the Lepchas to further westwards into the country of the Limboos, and this latter further to the west. The ruins of forts built by the Mangars, called Dzongs, are still found in many parts of Sikkim (Gurung; 2011).

The astounding similarity in the numerical system of the Lepcha and Mangar languages like Nat, Nees, Som, Buli etc. not only indicate influence on each other but it is also a proof that these two communities lived together side by side in the ancient past. The Mangars share some religious, cultural, and linguistic similarity with the Gurungs also. In Hooker's writing, Murmis (Tamangs) finds a special as one of the native tribes of Sikkim. He writes that the Murmis are the only other native tribe remaining in any numbers in Sikkim.

They are the scattered people of Tibetan origin and called 'Nishung' named after the two districts of Nimo and Shung, the places of their early inhabitation, situated on the way to Lhasa. They were originally called Bhote, meaning Tibetans, but later they assumed the title 'Tamang' indicating their traditional occupation as "horse riders". The word "Tamang", it is claimed, is derived from the Tibetan word 'Tamakh' meaning "mounted guard" of the king. In Tibetan language 'Ta' means 'horse' and 'Makh' means 'mounted guard'. In course of time the word 'makh' is believed to have been corrupted as 'Mang'. The Rai community, which is a consistent of the larger Kirata family, is also considered as the ancient inhabitants of Sikkim. A special reference to the Rai tribal community as a contemporary of the Lepchas is found in the writings of W.G. Mackean. Chaudhuri also writes that the Rais have come to Sikkim along with the Lepchas from the Assam hills. A.C. Sinha writes, "in Sikkim there are three main sub-cultural stocks" of the Nepalis community namely "the Kiratas, the Newaris and the Gorkhas". Among the Kiratis, the Limboos, the Rais, the Lepchas, the Gurungs, the

Tamangs and the Mangars constitute the autochthonous inhabitants of Sikkim. He further adds that with the growing assertion of the Bhotia rulers, the Limboos, the Mangars, the Lepchas and other Kirati tribes were pushed westward to Nepal and southwards to India. Risley also writes "The Limboos, Gurungs (Tamus), Murmis, Khambus (Rais/Zimdars), and Mangars are allied, while the others, excepting the Lepcha and Bhutia, are later immigrants from beyond the Arun in Nepal. According to Haimendrof in his classic work 'Himalayan Traders' has described Gurungs and the Rais as tribal communities of Sikkim. The Gurungs of Chakung are called Taksari Gurung and were associated with copper mining. In 1891 the Gurung community constituted the fourth largest community of Sikkim after the Lepchas, Bhutias and Limboos.

Risley, while reflecting on the population of Sikkim in 1891, had used different nomenclature, such as Rai, Khambu and Jimdar, considering each one as separate community but they belong to a single community, i.e., Khambu, the inhabitants of Khambuan.

It is said that after the occupation of the Khambuan by the Prithvi Narayan Shah in 1832, the Khambu tribal chief was given honorific title 'Rai'. 'Jimdar', on the other hand, is a corrupted version of the word 'Jimmadar' or 'Jimmidar' or 'Jamindar' (landlords) which probably means the 'functionary with official responsibility' (Jimma = custody or hold + Dar = custodian or holder of land). Taken both the Khambus and the Rai/Jimdar together, the community formed the largest constituent among the Nepali community in 1891 and continues to be so even in present day Sikkim. Presently, only the Rai community uses the title Kirata though etymologically it also includes Limboos, Gurung, Mangar, Tamang, Sunuwar, Lepchas.

The bulk of the Nepalis, particularly those belonging to the Aryan stock, appear to have migrated in the middle of the 19th century. Scholars like T.B. Subba relate the migration with the territorial conquests. He explains that a large chunk of territory of Sikkim, i.e., eastward of Mechi river to the westward of Teesta River, was under the Nepal for about thirty-seven years since 1780. Many Nepalese living in that territory is known to have come and settled in Sikkim since then. Not only Sikkim, but the present day also Tarai belt consisting of Siliguri and adjoining areas was permanently inhabited by the Nepalis and Adhibashi people, there is no record of the Bengali population in Siliguri. In fact, the name Siliguri itself is originated from the stone fort constructed by the Gorkha Army at the time of invasion of Sikkim.

Secondly, the scholars like P.K. Rao and B.S.K. Grover consider that Nepalese were particularly encouraged to settle in Sikkim by the British for two important reasons: (a) to accelerate the economic growth and (b) to counteract the supremacy of the Sikkimese royal family and the Bhutia councilors. Yet other scholars like Karan and Jenkins, Lall and, later, Datta Ray consider J. Claude White, the first British political officer of Sikkim, predominantly responsible for the large-scale migration of the Nepalese.

Before assuming his new administrative responsibility in Sikkim as the political officer, J.C. White had spent a year or so in Nepal and thus had the experience of working and understanding the Nepali way of life. He justified the Nepali migration on the economic ground saying that "the un-enterprising, lazy and unthrifty aborigines would not respond to the strong inducements held out to them to open up this new land". In the administrative report of 1905-06 he writes, "The Nepali ryot is hardworking and thrifty as a rule, pays his taxes regularly and at the same time is a law-abiding and intelligent settler". In 1906 he expressed his willingness to open hitherto forbidden north district for the Nepalese in the interest of Sikkim. During 1910-11 he regretted that "immigration from Nepal continues but not on as large a scale as formerly". Equally responsible were those Lepchas councilors and landlords who always favored settlement of Nepalese in Sikkim for economic benefits. The prominent among them were Tseepa Lama, Khangsa Dewan, Phodong Lama and Lasso Athing. (REF) (Gurung; 2011).

Apart from the economic reason, there is a political dimension also associated with the process of migration. In the context of Sikkim, the British interest had always met fitting challenges from the pro-Tibetan forces within Sikkim and Tibet as a whole. Sikkim, in fact, proved to be a common bone of contention between the British and the Tibetan rulers. The Tibetan had always considered Sikkim as an extension of Tibet, and the successive Chogyals, except for Sir Tashi Namgyal, looked towards Tibet as an ultimate source of guidance in all respects, including management of monasteries and religious matters.

Thus, to combat against such a strong contender and challenger it was obvious for J.C. White to turn towards the Nepalese who had already proved their being sui generis both in times of war and peace. In this connection Basnet writes, "The Gorkas made as good a peasant in peace time as he made a soldier in war. The Bhutias and Lepchas made poor farmers partly because of a natural indolence. The Lepchas had always been used to easy going ways and was averse to hard labor or, for that matter, any other form of strife and struggle.

The Bhutias, while having natural aptitude for trade, was loath to physical labor. Another factor which seemed to have worked for Nepalese was the changing socio-political scenario in the Himalayan kingdom. The military expeditions intending to consolidate Nepal politically under Prithvi Narayan Saha and his successors, the population explosion, and its effect on land holdings, declining economic conditions and food deficiency in Nepal are especially highlighted by scholars as indigenous factors, also called push factors, responsible for Nepali migration.

Whereas various treaty agreements such as Anglo-Nepalese friendship treaty of 1850, the Indo-Nepal Peace and Friendship Treaty of 1950 etc. served as legal political framework in the process of migration and are considered external factors or pull factors.

For instance, Article 7 of the Indo-Nepal Treaty of 1950 states; "The government of India and Nepal agree to grant, on a reciprocal basis, to the nationals of one country in the territories of the other the same privileges in the matter of residence, ownership of property, participation in trade and commerce, movement and other privileges of a similar nature" (Gurung; 2011).

Another element, which should be taken into cognizance, is that all Nepalese who have settled in Sikkim might not be migrants from places of Nepal. As mentioned earlier many tribal communities, who are presently included into the Nepali fold, inhabited the western and southern parts of Sikkim long before the country got its present name. Sikkim of the 18th or 19th centuries cannot be considered as the land of economic opportunity or socio-politically enticing for settlement purposes. Thus, many groups who were known by their own individual calling were living in Sikkim from the very early days, but the term Nepali is of later origin. They are so used to their individual calling that even today during the census enumeration they err by writing group's title instead of Nepali.

According to the unconfirmed report the Nepalis were perhaps 1995 persons in 1840 out of a total population of 7000 persons. According to Edgar the total population of Sikkim in 1873 was 5000 persons out of which Nepalis, including the Limboos, were 1000. The populations gradually increased with the passage of time and under various historical/political circumstances.

Nepalese are predominantly Hindus by religion and linguistically different from that of the Bhutias or Lepchas. For being one of the premier communities of Sikkim, they assert their own separate identity and resent any propaganda undermining their interest and existence/ identity. The Bhutias, on the other, are apprehensive about the Nepalese because of their numbers, economic well-being, and assertive nature.

In her article, Chie Nakane attempts to highlight areas of disagreement by saying that "ruling class (Bhutias) of Sikkim is much concerned, not only about the Nepali economic exploitation of the Lepchas and the Bhutia community, but also about the increase of the Nepali population as opposed to the decrease of the Lepchas-Bhutia population." Nepalese seemed to have shown great resilience despite the use or misuse of legal political apparatus against the community in the past. The differential treatment against the community strengthened the feeling of togetherness or belongingness among various sections of Nepalese, on the one hand, and emergence of new class of educated individuals, on the other. These new breeds of Nepalese were not only employed in various governmental capacities but were also active in the field of politics and were at the helm of corridors of power.

In 1941 the first ever social organization of the Nepalis, called Member Party, was born at Namthang with the objectives to oppose the oppressive rules and the practice of forced labour, called Zharlangi. Later in 1947, three other socio-political organizations by the name of Praja Sudharak Samaj, Praja Sammelan and Praja Mandal were born predominantly led or with the support of the Nepalese. In 1948 these three organizations were merged to form a full-fledged political party by the name of Sikkim State Congress with objectives to abolition of Zamindari system, formation of interim government and accession of Sikkim with India.

After the establishment of a democratic government in India in 1947 Sikkim entered into an interim agreement with India in 1948 and a fully-fledged treaty in 1950. With the signing of these treaty agreements the prospects for extension of democratic values in Sikkim became a reality. Gradually changes in old laws and system of governance had been introduced accommodating the interests of Nepalese. In 1951 six seats were reserved for the Nepalese in the state council which was further raised to 16 in 1974. In 1975 Sikkim was merged with India and with it the Nepali seats had been converted into 17 general seats in 1979.

Nepali language became one of the official languages in 1977 though the languages had been the lingua-franca of the state from the very early days. The first ever coin minted in Sikkim in 1880s was engraved in Nepali. The first Nepali boarding school was set up at Gangtok in 1906 which in 1925 was merged with Bhutia boarding school to form Tashi Namgyal High School of the present day. In 1921 Nepali language was used as the medium of instruction in this school and in the following year it became an optional paper and compulsory paper since 1924. From 1925 Nepali became the medium of instructions in all the schools of Sikkim. At present, apart from Nepali, languages spoken by various other constituents of the larger Nepali community like Newar, Gurung, Rai, Sunuwar, Mangar, Limboo, and Tamang languages have been recognized as official languages and are taught at the school and undergraduate levels in Sikkim.

Nepalese in Sikkim are classified into four groups namely scheduled tribes (limboos and Tamangs), most backward classes (Gurungs, Rai, Mangar, Thami, Sunuwar, Bhujel, Dewan etc.), other backward classes (Bahuns, Chettris, and Newars) and scheduled castes (Kami, Damai, Sarki etc.). Many languages and dialects are spoken in Sikkim. The three main languages of the state are Nepali spoken by about 90% of the population, Bhutia about 28% and the Lepchas about 10%. Various other dialects of ancient Nepali tribes which are in use are Gurung, Limbu, Kharabu, Mangari and Murmi. The Lepchas and Bhutia speak their own language though many of them can understand and speak Nepali. Hindi is generally understood by most of the people. Lamaism, Hinduism, and Animism are practiced by different ethnic groups. Some Nepalis are Hindus and others are Buddhist. Lepchas are animist, Buddhist and Christians. Bhutias are mainly Buddhists but now we find in some places Bhutias being converted to Christians. And the religion of the Scheduled Castes is uncertain, but we can find their inclination towards Hinduism (Gurung; 2011).

Conclusion

When we try to see the ethnic groups of Sikkim from the historical times till date, we find ample numbers of transformations in Sikkim from the ancient times and till date. Off Late, we have been even realizing the ongoing or changing dynamics between ethnic groups of Sikkim.

For instance, if we trace out right from the beginning of the ancient times, i.e., the way the indigenous people (Lepchas) were ruled by the Bhutia king after migrating from Tibet. Eventually how the early inhabitants got subsumed after the establishment of the monarchic theocratic system. Above all, the whole notion about the early inhabitants or the autochthone of Sikkim is still in dilemma as to who were the ones.

Later, after the migration of Nepalis to Sikkim, due to various reasons, this in a way slowly paved a way to form a multi-ethnic society in Sikkim. It was only after various struggles and demands for the removal of monarchy and the idea of democracy got established in 1975, after being merged with the Indian union.

Again now, we see the various sub-groups within the Nepali group itself. Nevertheless, we can say that since Sikkim as a state consists of three major ethnic groups like Lepchas, Bhutia, and Nepali. Thus, it can be said that Sikkim is a multi-ethnic state. But if we see deep inside, we find many possibilities of conflict within these three major ethnic groups of Sikkim.

For instance, some groups try to maintain and emerge themselves and create a different identity. The issues like the demands by the Nepali for the reservation in state legislative assembly. But still, we find fewer antagonisms between the ethnic groups.

If we see many of the ethnic violence in many parts of the country and state, we find Sikkim as a state which consists of multi-ethnic diversity is successful in maintaining peace. Therefore, the forces/mechanisms which lead to the maintenance of ethnic-Peace in Sikkim need to be paid attention in further sustaining it.

THREE

RELATIONS AMONG DIFFERENT ETHNIC COMMUNITIES: A HISTORICAL ANALYSIS

CHAPTER III

RELATIONS AMONG DIFFERENT ETHNIC COMMUNITIES: A HISTORICAL ANALYSIS

This chapter tries to examine the ethnic relations among the three major ethnic communities in Sikkim and tries to discuss the mechanisms through which ethnic harmony had been maintained. The chapter also looks at the different periods of Sikkim's history and how a composite, multicultural society was developed subsequently. The discussion in the previous chapter about the major ethnic groups in Sikkim and their history illustrates how during time Sikkim developed as a multi-ethnic society. There are numerous cases in the world where there is ethnic violence like ethnic conflict in Srilanka, Yugoslavia and closer home, in many parts of the North-Eastern states of India itself. Sikkim, despite the multiplicity of communities, has been successful in maintaining peace so far.

SIKKIM: AN ACCOUNT OF ANCIENT SOCIAL STRUCTURE

It is generally believed that the first political system evolved in Sikkim by the Lepchas was a patriarchal one. People were divided into various political classes, which were believed to have originated in some supernatural or legendary ancestor. A class was under a chieftain. A local lord exercised control over several classes. The overall authority, though in a loose form, was vested in a king (Panu). The spiritual side of the Lepchas was taken care of by four major spirits – Mun, Padam, Yaba, and Pau. The priestly class was supposed to have possessed these spirits. But the highest spirit, the Mun, was believed to be possessed by the rulers. Thus, both the temporal as well as spiritual authority was exercised by the leaders who happened to be elderly and venerated persons. This indigenous system and the independence of the Lepchas continued to operate in Sikkim behind the barrage of snowy peaks and thick jungles till the beginning of the seventeenth century, when the persecution of the red-sect Buddhists by the yellow-sect led a large number of Tibetans to take refuge in Sikkim. (Bhadra 1992, pp.75-76)

When the Tibetans arrived in Sikkim the central authority of king (Panu) was, however declining and every clan under its leader was breaking away from the loose federation. There were frequent fights between various classes for the occupation of fertile valleys. Such a chaotic situation was favorable for the Tibetans to impose their rule in Sikkim. The Tibetans had stronger culture, social and political institutions, and leadership, compared to those of Lepchas. After completing the occupation, they started converting the Lepchas to Buddhism. When a substantial number of the Lepchas were converted, the Tibetans established temporal authority over them. With it began a new era in the political history of Sikkim.

The political system established by the Tibetan settlers was based on an agreement according to which the Lepchas were to be treated as equals although political authority was to be in the hands of the Tibetan ruler. This agreement was not acceptable to a section of the Lepchas who had not been converted to Buddhism, and, therefore, a war ensued between this section of the Lepchas and the Tibetans, culminating in another agreement according to which the temporal power was shared with a Lepchas chief. But gradually the Tibetans were able to extend their authority throughout Sikkim and ultimately, they assumed both the temporal as well as the spiritual power. Thus, the way was clear for the introduction of Tibetan monarchy in Sikkim.

The majority of the Bhutia inhabitants are descendants of immigrants from Tibet and Bhutan in the 17th century who played an important role in establishing the kingdom of Sikkim. The majority included traders, peasants, and Buddhist monks as well as aristocrats who helped in the formation of kingdom and Tibetanization of the Lepchas. The Lepchas were shy and peace-loving people who avoided aggression in any form. Tibetan Bhutias were attracted to Sikkim's vast empty land, green valleys, rich forests, ample water supply and good climate in comparison to cold climate, their bare and inhospitable mountain plateau. Valleys of South Sikkim are favorable for the cultivation of rice. Tibetans who migrated into Sikkim in the thirteenth century started amalgamating with the indigenous population of Lepchas and practically assimilated in the course of time. The Lepchas who were animists were attracted by the rich Buddhist religion and cultural tradition of Bhutias. The area was resource rich, and Lepchas were less apprehensive of being dispossessed. Intermarriages of Lepcha - Bhutia resulted in the formation of Sikkimese Bhutia. (Bhasin 2002, p.4)

A bureaucratic kingdom was established by the immigrant Bhutias with the help of local chiefs. For administrative purpose, Sikkim was divided into 12 *Dzongs* (districts). Each Dzong had a Lepcha *Dzongpan* (governor), with a council of 12 ministers. For revenue collection, the whole state was divided into 104 estates, of these 15 estates form the private estate of the *Maharajah* and 5 estates were used for the upkeep of five big monasteries of Sikkim (Bhadra 1992, pp.76-77).

The Bhutia rule gave rise to a new social class called the *Kazis* who were barons with fifty to hundred villages and large tracts of forest under their administration. The *Kazi* collected the taxes and in turn paid a fixed sum calculated at a certain rate per acre to the king, the rate varying according to the condition of the estate. Even the *Kazi* had no proprietary right in the land, though he had a kind of hereditary title to his office. The *Kazi* or the landlord appointed a village *(Busti)* head man or *Mondol* who could rent out the arable land to the individual households. The political system of Sikkim was laid down following the system of Tibet - a kind of centralized feudal bureaucracy. Through the development of the power of the royal family, Bhutia aristocracy was taking form. There were 14 major Bhutia families of high rank grouped into two different descent groups (Gazetteer of Sikkim, 1894), to one belonged the group of royal family.

The initial clashes and conflicts between Lepcha-Bhutia disappeared almost completely due to cultural and social integration through intermarriages and ritual blood brotherhood with Lepcha chiefs. The Lepchas, though numerically dominant group was no threat to Bhutia's domination. Lepchas were no competitors for the resources as Bhutias preferred higher elevations in North and North Eastern part while Lepchas were forest dwellers practicing shifting cultivation along with hunting and gathering. The immigrant Bhutias were mostly traders, herdsmen, peasants, and monks. As Lepchas were practicing shifting cultivation, they were not particularly interested in owning land. In case of permanent settlers, the right of farmers on land, although similar were less transitory and allowed for alienation.

After the establishment of Bhutia bureaucracy the ownership of the cultivable land came under the control of mainly Bhutia landlords and aristocracy in the name of the *Maharajah*. As most of the Lepchas were tenant cultivators, the monopoly over the land resources shifted hands from the Lepchas to the Bhutias. Even then, anyone could open-up new land without any official permission.

Lepchas continued to practice shifting cultivation till the immigration of Nepalis. As the area was resource rich there was no confrontation between Bhutia and Lepcha over resources. However, along with establishment of kingdom spread of Tibetan-Buddhism was of equal significance.

BRITISH COLONIALISM AND NEPALI MIGRATION AND CHANGING SOCIAL FABRIC OF SIKKIM

Historically, the colonization of Nepalis in Sikkim was stimulated by the weakening of the political power of the Sikkim against Nepal during the latter part of the 15th century, and the strengthening of British political power in Sikkim since the 19th century. British favored the opening of the waste land of Sikkim to Nepali settlers. Nepalis' immigration was encouraged as labour was needed for construction of roads and extension of agriculture. The ethnic scene of Sikkim changed rapidly with the multiplication of the number of Nepalis. By 1981, the Nepalese had multiplied to 51% of the total population, thus reducing the Lepchas and the Bhutias to nineteen and sixteen per cent, respectively. The Nepali immigrants settled in Western and Southern part of Sikkim, as Nepali immigrants were prohibited (in response to ruling Bhutias plea) to settle on land in possession of Bhutia and Lepcha. They could only open uninhabited waste lands in parts of West and South Sikkim. They were not allowed to become headman and obtain any power as officers, which should always be entrusted to either Lepcha or Bhutia. By second half of the nineteenth century, the Sikkim court was losing its authority and Nepali immigration was allowed in a big way. In 1888, the first British Political Officer, J.C. White modified lease system of land tenure which resulted into emergence of some early Nepali settlers as lessee landlords known as *Thikkedars*. Among them were Newar or Pradhan families who worked as contractual landlords, miners, and minters for the Sikkim court. (Bhasin 2002, p.5)

The British administration, since the late nineteenth century, had encouraged the Nepalis to migrate into Sikkim in large numbers. The Nepalis could settle in the fertile southern valleys by indiscriminate clearing of forests. As the immigration continued with increasing pace during this period, the Nepalis far outnumbered the original Lepchas-Bhutia population. Therefore, the clearing of the forests by the Nepalis adversely affected the Lepchas-Bhutia interests. (Bhadra 1992, p.74)

The British created a landlord class from among the Nepalis, who wielded parallel economic power with the Lepchas-Bhutia Kazis. Under British patronage the Nepalis started accumulating landed assets which threatened the economic power of Kazis as also the livelihood prospects of the Lepchas-Bhutia commoners. On severe protest from these communities the British administration had to protect from Nepalis economic aggression. To this end there was an attempt to prevent land alienation by the Lepchas and Bhutia communities.

Revenue Order No. 1 of 1917 prohibited land alienation by the Bhutias and the Lepchas in favor of a person of another community without express permission of the State Government. Civil Courts were also debarred from sanctioning sales of land belonging to the Bhutia-Lepchas communities in favor of persons of the other communities in execution proceedings without the prior express sanction of the Government. By a later notification settlement of a person of another community in which was abandoned by a person of the Bhutia-Lepchas communities was prohibited, unless there was prior express permission of the Government. (Bhadra 1992, p.74)

By the above provisions the Lepchas and the Bhutias were settled in central and Northern Sikkim, on steeper hill slopes with less productive agricultural prospects than in South. These settlements were declared as reserve areas. In this context, the specification of 'location, extent and other particulars' relating to land transfer referred to in the Land Reforms Act becomes relevant.

The Sikkimese identity came into existence particularly after the *Durbar* (during the regime of *Chogyal*) recognized the earlier settlers as legal settlers who had been given the status of subjects of Sikkim which referred to as Sikkimese by Sikkim Subject Regulations, 1961. The Sikkim Ruling Durbar (12) maintained a register of all such legal settlers who were recognized as Sikkim subjects. A plot of land played a positive role for Nepalese to become eligible for State subject ship. (Bhasin 2002, pp.5-6).

This regulation excluded 70 percent of the Nepalese residing in the State, and included Lepcha, Bhutia and Tsongs (Limbus) as subjects of Sikkim state. The main purpose of this regulation was to preserve the economic and political interests of ruling elites and monopolize the resources. The act was modified on 16th Jan 1962, where in all reference to the communities was deleted from the Regulation.

Even then, the recognition of the Lepcha, the Bhutia and the Limbu as the citizen was automatic by virtue of being earlier settlers. But it was not easy for the early Nepali settlers to prove this. However, it was recognized in course of time and they were granted Sikkimese status. There were other discriminations regarding the land-tenure which favored only Lepcha-Bhutia. The lease of land was given to Nepali *Thikkedars* for ten years while it was for 15 years for *Kazis* (Rose, 1978: 215).

Besides a law was in force prohibiting land alienation by hereditary status subject (Bhutia-Lepcha) in favor of non-hereditary subjects e.g., Nepalese (Sengupta, 1985: 21). Even the land revenue for different ethnic groups was discriminatory. The Nepalis had to pay higher rent for the same area and same quality of land than the Bhutia-Lepcha. Because of these discriminations the Sikkimese society was bifurcated into two main ethnic groups - Bhutia Lepcha and the Nepali.

Later Sikkim became the 22nd state of India and the Indian Constitution was extended to Sikkim and the Sikkim Citizenship Order 1975 was issued by the Indian Government. According to this order, every person who immediately before the 26th day of April 1975 was a Sikkim subject under the Sikkim Subject Regulations, 1961 shall be deemed to have become a citizen of India on that day ' (Himalaya Today, June 1988). This made a sizeable number as non-Sikkimese. However, a compromised formula was designed for the election purpose and a sizable number of them acquired Indian Citizenship. Thereby, the identity as Sikkim subject, which previously included Bhutia-Lepcha, now included some Nepalis as well. Ethnic Groups and ethnic identities emerge as part of a social and political process.

It is believed that shared ethnic identity often makes people feel comfortable with similar people and give them a sense of belonging. However, ethnic differences in multi-ethnic societies are usually associated with inequalities in resource sharing, power and prestige and results in stratification of the society.

Demographically in contemporary Sikkim, the Buddhists comprise a large minority of 27 per cent while 68 per cent of its total population are Hindus and 3 per cent are "converted" Christians with some Muslims who settled recently [Census2001]. The majorities of the Hindus of Sikkim have ethnic-national origins in neighboring Nepal and considered to be migrants by the indigenous

Lepchas-Bhutias (20.6 per cent) who define themselves as the Sikkimese. Ethnically Sikkim's population is categorized into three groups: the Lepchas, the Bhutias and the Nepalis. There are cultural, religious, and linguistic differences between the Lepcha-Bhutia and the Nepalis that provide the objective basis for the ethnic boundaries between them. These broad categorizations underplay the competing definitions, the internal variations, and the intersections between the diverse ethnic groups in Sikkim. The main ethnic boundary is between the Lepchas and the Bhutias who are united in their opposition towards ethnic groups categorized as Nepali and termed as migrants by them. The Lepcha-Bhutia ethnic alliance has a historical, politico-economic, religious, and cultural basis although both communities have their distinctive cultures and languages. Historically, the Lepchas and the Bhutias were the ruling groups in the kingdom of Sikkim although the Lepchas were and are a subordinate partner in this alliance. On the one hand, the Lepchas and the Bhutias instrumentally use the idiom of sacred landscapes to challenge and contest the belonging of Nepali groups in contemporary Sikkim, then on the other hand; the Nepalis cites their contribution towards developing Sikkim's economy in the last 150 years to assert their claims over the land and "belonging" in the landscape. The Nepalis continue to be blamed for causing civil unrest that culminated in Sikkim's incorporation into India in 1975. Ethnic relations are neither harmonious nor have ethnic tensions escalated into any secessionist demands or led to an insurgency. (Arora 2006, p.4064)

Clearly, conflict, negotiations, and integration occupy centre-stage as ethnic groups compete for scarce resources, demand reservation in government jobs, educational institutions, and preferential opportunities in development. The links between symbolic identity, livelihood, and ethnicity cannot be ignored in this multi-ethnic context. Identity politics and conflict over resource-entitlements establish the contours of fault lines in this Himalayan borderland.

SIKKIM IN THE POST 1947 PERIOD

To understand the political contours, ethnic-fissures, and cultural politics over resources in the present, hence, it is necessary to understand Sikkim's political history that led to its incorporation into India. Sikkim became a de jure and de facto protectorate of British India after the Young-husband mission of 1904 wherein the British raj defeated Tibet. The Government of India Act of 1935 recognized Sikkim to be a state of India and it was allocated a seat in the council of Indian states. However, in 1947 Sikkim chose not to merge into India although the king permitted India to station a political officer within Sikkim. On December 5, 1950, the Indo-Sikkim treaty was signed that confirmed Sikkim's protectorate status that conferred external affairs, defense, law and order and communication responsibilities on the government of India while the king of Sikkim retained autonomy in internal affairs. There is a large body of literature on whether Sikkim was merged into India or was annexed by India in 1975. The Chinese annexation of Tibet in 1959, the Sino-Indian war on Sikkim's border in 1962-63, the democratic aspirations of the population agitating against the oppressive rule of Sikkim's feudal oligarchy, and the breakdown of internal law and order are cited as reasons for holding the 1975 referendum, which culminated in the inclusion of Sikkim in India in 1975. Special provisions were inserted into the Indian Constitution under Article 371F to meet the special needs and circumstances of the state. According to Article 371F(f) the Parliament may, for the purpose of protecting the rights and interests of the different sections of the population of Sikkim make provisions for the number of seats in the legislative assembly of the state of Sikkim which may be filled by candidates belonging to such sections and for the delimitation of the assembly constituencies from which candidates belonging to such sections alone may stand for election to the legislative assembly of the state of Sikkim [Jain 2000: 989].

Sikkim's democratic polity does not have secular roots and some continuity with the theocratic rule of the Namgyal dynasty has been provided for in the Indian Constitution under Article 371F along with certain political safeguards that constitute representation to the Buddhist monasteries in its legislative assembly in the form of the Sangha seat even as it ensures the continued administration of monasteries and their preservation by the ecclesiastical department of the state government.

In 1978, the Lepchas and the Bhutias were recognized as scheduled tribes and 12 seats have been reserved in the legislative assembly to safeguard their political interests; quotas too were reserved for them in government employment and educational institutions. These safeguards were justified to protect the interests of the Lepchas and the Bhutias who were rendered a political minority with the incorporation of Sikkim into India. A few Nepali politicians (especially R C Poudyal) regarded these special provisions as being discriminatory and unconstitutional. They filed a petition in the Supreme Court of India in the early 1980s where it was hotly debated for more than a decade. Even in 1984, justice Bhagwati stated that under Article 371F (f) reservation of seats for the

Bhutias-Lepchas and the Sangha in the Sikkim assembly were justified [Kazi 1993: 128-31]. Therefore, the matter was kept pending until the Supreme Court (in a 3:2 decision by a five-member bench) made a landmark judgment on February 10, 1993 upholding the reservation of the Bhutia-Lepcha seats and one seat for the Sangha in the legislative assembly. This decisive judgment upheld the validity of the 36th Constitution (Amendment) Act 1975 which provided special status to ethnic and religious groups in Sikkim. Justice Venkatachaliah argued that "historical considerations justified a differential treatment" [Kazi 1993: 337]. The Supreme Court judgment of 1993 explicitly acknowledged that these provisions were necessitated since a nation was being incorporated into a state: It is true that the reservation of seats of the kind and the extent brought about by the impugned versions may not, if applied to the existing States of the Union, pass the Constitutional muster. But in relation to a new territory admitted to a Union, the terms and conditions are not such as to fall outside the permissible constitutional limits.

Historical considerations and compulsionsdo justify inequality and special treatment. We are of the viewthat the impugned provisions have been found in the wisdomof Parliament [that were] necessary in the admission of [a]strategic border state into the Union. The departures are not suchas to negate the principles of democracy [Kazi 1993: 338,emphasis added].

These special provisions were intended to overcome disruptions by ensuring a smoother integration of Sikkim into India while continuities with its theocratic heritage were maintained. Nonetheless the Supreme Court judgment of 1993 emphasized the transitional character of these provisions: The provisions of clause (f) of Article 371F

(f) and the consequent changes in the electoral laws were intended to recognize and accommodate the pace of the growth of the political institutions of Sikkim and to make the transition gradual and peaceful and to prevent the dominance of one section of the population over another based on ethnic loyalties and identities. These adjustments reflect the political expediencies for the maintenance of social equilibrium. The political and social maturity and of economic development might in course of time enable the people of Sikkim to transcend and submerge these ethnic apprehensions and imbalances and might in future – one hopes sooner – usher in a more egalitarian dispensation [Kazi 1993: 337-38].

DEMAND FOR STs AND ASSERTION OF KIRANTI IDENTITY

The recent inclusion of the Limbu and the Tamang in the scheduled tribe category in 2002 has evoked bitter opposition from the Lepchas and the Bhutias who resent the dilution of their indigeneity and are not prepared to share their entitlements with other groups. This provides the context for debating these special provisions and revisiting them. The Limboos and Tamangs are demanding political reservation similar to what is provisioned for the Lepchas and the Bhutias in the Constitution. Currently, the Sikkim government has proposed to the central government that the strength of the state legislative assembly be increased from 32 to 40 seats to give the Limboos and the Tamangs the benefit of their tribal status.

In the census of 2001, the Limboos and the Tamangs were enumerated as part of the Nepali population. Currently, these groups are demanding a fresh census enumeration which acknowledges their categorization as scheduled tribes to assert and ascertain their exact numerical strength and thereby legitimize their demand for a proportionate share in reserved seats for their political representatives, jobs in government employment, and seats in educational institutions. The Lepchas are demanding "primitive tribe" status while some other Nepali groups such as the Khambu Rai, Gurung, Mangar, Sunwar, Thami, Dewan and Bhujel are pressurizing the state government and the National Commission of Backward Classes to include them in the list of scheduled tribes. (Arora 2006, pp.4064-4066).

The belated step to label the Limboos as one of the OBCs did not satisfy their expectations. In fact, the community was nursing a grievance against the democratic dispensation, which had lumped it along with rest of the Nepamul for political representation. They even fondly remembered that the Buddhist segment among them (the *Tshongs*) was allotted a seat in the State Council in 1967, which was done away with in 1974. Thus, they continued to press for recognition of their status as a scheduled tribe, as they claimed to be the original Kirat inhabitants of Sikkim along with Lepchas and Magars. At last, in December 2002, Limboos and Tamangs were accorded the status of the Scheduled Tribes in Sikkim and West Bengal. Furthermore, in partial modification of earlier orders of the State through the Notification No.2/WD of June 2, 1994 and Notification No. 236/SW/251(3) WD dated June 15, 2000, the Government of Sikkim declared (i) Bhujel, (ii) Dewan, (iii) Gurung, (iv) Jogi, (v) Kirat Rai, (vi) Magar, (vii) Sunuwar, and (viii) Thami as the "Most Backward Classes, MBC". Similarly, (I) Bahun, (ii) Chhetri, (iii) Newar, and (IV) Sanyasi were given the status of "Other Backward Classes, OBC" in Sikkim (Vide Sikkim Government Gazette: Extraordinary, No. 308 dated Gangtok, Friday 19th September 2003). In this context, the readers may be reminded of a news item in the Gangtok Times, informing formation of a 'Bahun-Chhetri- Newar Association' with avowed objective of "protecting unity of the Sikkimese People" on the plea that though some of them were considered 'forward', but most of the members of the castes were poor and 'have-nots' (The Gangtok Times: Vol. 2 (no.16), dated April 29-May 4, 1995).

By these notifications P K Chamling the CM had fulfilled the promises made in 1996 to the State to bring every Nepamul community under OBC quota. It may be noted that the State Assembly has 12 seats reserved for the Lepcha- Bhutia communities, and not for the Scheduled Tribes as elsewhere in India, a provision, which was challenged in the court of law. The highest court in India, the Supreme Court, upheld the provision as a part of the "Tripartite Agreement" signed on May 8, 1973 between the then ruler, representative of the Union Government and representatives of the political parties in Sikkim. Now, that the Limbu and Tamang, who have been recognized as the Scheduled Tribes, and they naturally demand political representation in State Assembly as elsewhere in the country, which has remained an enigma. Apparently, 12 seats reserved for the Lepcha- Bhutia by name cannot be shared with anybody, even with the scheduled tribes, and there is no seat set aside for the Scheduled Tribes in the Assembly. The Government of Sikkim has come out with various suggestions to solve the problem, but way out has not been found by now. This has not deterred many other communities from the Most Backward Classes or the MBCs from staking claims to be lumped among the omnibus ancient Kirat band bagan. As many eight ethnic groups (Bhujel, Dewan, Gurung, Jogi, Magar, Rai, Sunuwar and Thami) with the claim of being ancient Kirat tribes impressed upon the Government of Sikkim to accord them the status of the Scheduled Tribes. This earnestness is partly based among the claimants on the false assumption that the status of Scheduled tribe will ensure their representation in the State Assembly. Some way or other, the Government of Sikkim saw the merit in their claims and approached the Union Government to accord its approval, but they were advised to re-apply for the consideration along with an 'ethnographic report on the claims of the various communities'. The Government of Sikkim did that by the earliest by appointing a Committee1 of four Experts headed by Prof. A C Sinha with an historian (Prof. J P Singh) and two anthropologists (Prof. T B Subba and Prof. S R Mandal) as members, to prepare an ethnographic report on the said communities' claim within 100 days. The Committee submitted its Report to the state government in the middle of 2005 (Sinha 2009).

The Government of Sikkim sent the report to the Ministry of Home Affairs, Government of India without its own recommendations, which did not find favor with the Union Government once more. Then state Government came out with another idea to appoint a seven-member Commission headed by an anthropologist, B K Ray Burman in December 2005 for the purpose 2. The Commission has held a series of seating in and outside Sikkim and submitted its Report in September 2008.

Coming to the Committee's Report, prior to approaching the Union Government in 2004, the Government of Sikkim asked their concerned officials to request the community organizations of the MBCs to prepare their respective ethnographic reports. In terms of their demographic size, some of them are in thousands, for example, Rais have many as 72, 418 individuals as per the last census conducted in 2001. Gurung (37, 105) and Magar (10, 858) are other two numerically important communities. However, there are as many as five communities between 3, 326 (Bhujel) to as less as 223 (Thami). Six of the communities (Bhujel, Dewan, Gurung, Kirat Rai, Magar and Sunuwar) presented their respective reports for the consideration of the appointed Committee for the purpose. It is interesting to learn that even the officers of the Department of Social Welfare, Government of Sikkim failed to locate any social or welfare organization among two of the numerically smaller communities (Jogi and Thami) and thus, there was no 'report' presented to the Committee on their behalf. There was a 'report' on behalf of Dewans, but no community with this nomenclature is known to the Indian Census Operation.

Three of the communities, Magar, Sunuwar and Rai, had published their history and ethnography in the recent past. The first two did it in Nepali and last one in English. It is apparent that a great deal of expectations has been created among the communities and nobody wants to miss this opportunity to be listed among the Scheduled Tribes. And, no doubt, the respective associations of the various communities went out to look afresh on their unique customs, dress, food item and habit, art, craft, architect, vocations, implements, ornaments, marital pattern, and anything, which was exclusive to them and earnestly recorded in their reports.

However, even a casual probing reveals that cultural traits claimed to be uniquely special attribute of the claimed community is shared with the neighbors. Perhaps in the words of sociologist of culture, Bennett M Berger, they "want to assert, argue, persuade that such symbols/ meanings, like baskets, pots, and watches, are about getting us through the days and nights we are more or less stuck with, and in doing so providing us with a sense of having got through with some dignity_ itself, of course, is a precious piece of culture...that to see the matter this way is not to demean (de-mean) the dignity; it is only to look it hard in the face, and ask it tough questions"(Berger, B M : 1995:8-9).

Reading these Reports gives the impression that all these communities were descendants of the ancient Kiratas or Kirants; they were forced by the Hindu kings and the Brahmin priests to follow Sanskritic traditions and Brahminical rituals. All of them emphasized their differences with other fellow Kiratas. Again, all of them, with exception of Jogi, claim to speak distinct dialects of their own. But pressed for information as to whether they speak the claimed tongue at home, it was found that all of them speak Nepali among themselves at home as the mother tongues. However, State has recognized their languages as official languages and some token teachers have been appointed to teach them in some of the schools. But there are no pupils around to teach and in many cases the textbooks are yet to be produced and written. Interestingly, most of them inter-marry among the communities claiming Kirat nomenclature. Their rite de passage exhibits a common pattern along with other caste Hindus in terms of rituals and other personal effects. Many of the communities have their own sacred specialists, but they invite Brahmin priests on the eve of marriage and death rituals. Most of these communities face the problem of a mixed settlement with communities not necessarily of the eastern Himalayan region. "The Kiratas of the eastern Himalayas are today suffering from a lack of national symbols which would represent them and simultaneously differentiate them from the Tagadharis and Untouchables, whose culture is so like that of the Tagadharis. The question of difference with Other Mongoloids is perhaps the most vexing one for various reasons.

It is important for the Kiratas to construct powerful symbol of differences with the Tagadharis for it is mainly the latter that they hold responsible for their present situation. It is again the latter against whom they occur to be fighting. But this fight is uneasy: the symbol of difference between them are not so powerful as the Kirata leaders would like them to be...other facts of their lives and living such as economic interdependence, language, dress, ecology, and destiny bind them together rather than separate them. Retreating to an ideal and convenient past to construct the symbol of difference is common but in no way easy for the Kiratas" (Subba, T B: 1999: 106).

The above quote is to a great extent out of mark in Sikkimese situation, as the Kiratas are already in power and they do control the lever of authority as per law of the land. In fact, the Bhutias did incorporate a section of the Limbu in their fold through the mechanism of 'lhomontshong', a cultural commonwealth of Bhutias, Lepchas and the Tshongs (Sinha, A C: 1975).

Ethnicity is nothing, but a myth of collective ancestry, which usually carries with it the traits believed to be innate. Immigrants from Nepal to Sikkim had a mixed heritage, divided into castes and tribes. And there was hardly a village, which entirely belonged to one community alone. First as the 'Paharias' and then as the "Nepalese', they had to suffer against the feudal oppression in the Buddhist kingdom of Sikkim ruled by a Bhutia king. The immigrants were treated as hewers of the wood and drawers of the water for landed gentry, which was largely Buddhist Kazis

They, had to pay a higher rate of land rent in cash compared to the older subjects of the principality, who paid it in kind. They were subjected to a series of exploitative labour obligations in form of **Kurwa, Bethi, Jharlangi, Kalobhari**. Against all these oppressions, they stood together in their Nepali dress, converse in their lingua franca, Nepali and it were the ill-educated and invariably self-taught roving Brahmin priests, who helped them to keep their body and soul together with the help of ritual performance, singing the mythologies, and reminding them of their 'karma' in this birth.

They had pride to be 'Nepalese', who were known as the fighters, and they were fighting the unequal and unjust feudal system, which was deliberately tilted against them. In a way, this fight came to an end in 1975, when the feudal dispensation came to an end and they tried to choose a series of identities available to them with a view to appropriating certain resources (Sinha, A C: 1981).

Since then, Nepamul Bharatiyas are engaged in a different kind of struggle. And this struggle is addressed to finding an honourable place in Indian political system. First, they fought for recognition of their language, Nepali as an Indian language, getting citizenship rights to the left-over Nepamul Sikkimese and separate seats, reserved for them in the state legislative assembly. They succeeded in first two and are trying to maneuver the third one. If you cannot beat the system, you join it; and that's what they have decided to do now by taking advantage of the constitutional provisions of providing special treatment to the "educationally, economically and socially backward communities". In the light of that one may appreciate ethnic rush for "Kirat identity" among discrete communities. This move poses fewer problems for the

Lamaist communities from the Kiratis such as Limbus, Tamangs and Gurungs, but for the rest such as Rais, Magar, Sunuwar etc, it also amounts to distancing from Hinduism to certain extent. However, the consolation is that "Hinduism works as an integrative factor for the whole of the Hindu society only for so long as the lower castes accept the legitimacy of their own position. Even in the past that acceptance was never total, and it does not exist today" (Whelpton, John: 1997:92). Right now, society in Sikkim presents an image of fragmented entity, divided communally and ethnically. Is it real situation or postures adopted for the purpose on the occasion to appropriate political, economic, and social space? The above quote in the beginning appears to remind the past mind set of the community, which is now aiming for new possibilities within the Indian constitutional framework (Sinha 2009).

Early response of the Government of Sikkim to the cause of social justice is that the, coming to Sikkimese situation, the Government of India had issued the Scheduled Tribe and Scheduled Caste Order notifying Bhutias and Lepchas as Scheduled Tribes and Damai, Kami, Manjhi and Saraki as the Scheduled Castes on June 26, 1978. (Sinha 2009)

The Bill No. 9 (for rearranging seats in the State Legislative Assembly in Sikkim) was introduced in the Lok Sabha on May 18, 1979, which became an Act in 1981 during the Prime Minister ship of late Mrs. Indira Gandhi. This parliamentary provision had 12 seats reserved for the minority Lepcha –Bhutia communities (termed as the Scheduled Tribes), 2 seats for the Scheduled Castes and 1 for the monasteries (the *Sangha*) and remaining 17 were declared 'General' in which any Indian who is a bona fide voter in Sikkim can be elected. Keeping in mind that the Lepcha –Bhutias have distinct culture and traditions, they have been treated as the Scheduled Tribes under Article 342 of the Indian Constitution (Kazi, J N: 1994: 339). It is very pertinent to remember that elsewhere in India seats in the legislative bodies have been reserved for the Scheduled tribes of the state or the districts, but in case of Sikkim an exception has been made by mentioning Lepcha-Bhutia by name. Similarly, considering the unique role-played by the Buddhist monks and monasteries in the body politic of Sikkim in the past, secular India made a special provision to allot a seat to the monastic bodies, Sangha in the State Legislative.

Nar Bahadur Bhandari's third term as the Chief Minister of Sikkim from 1989 onwards marked the gradual integration of Sikkim with Indian political system. The Government of India had decided to implement the recommendation of the Backward Class Report by reserving 27 percent seats in educational, welfare, and political and administrative offices to the communities listed by the Commission as the backward. Incidentally, the said Commission had listed all the communities in Sikkim as economically and educationally backward. Naturally, Sikkim could not remain untouched from this development.

The Chief Minister Bhandari, hailing from the Chhetri caste, instead of responding positively to the demand of the Other Backward Classes (OBCs), was busy spearheading a demand for the recognition of the Nepali language as one of the Indian national languages. One of his longtime associates, Pawan Kumar Chamling hailing from Rai community, and a cabinet minister, raised the issue of implementing the recommendations of the Mandal Commission Report in Sikkim in 1992 and for that he was expelled from the Sikkim Sangram Parishad (S S P)

Legislative Party. However, within a few months, a turning point came in 1994, when the State Assembly passed the resolution against the implementation of the Mandal Commission Report. Within no time 19 out of 31 members of Bhandari's Legislative Party deserted him to form a parallel political forum, Sikkim Sangram Parishad (Sanchman). Bhandari was voted out of the office of the Chief Minister on May 19, 1994. The successor government immediately recommended to the Union Government to include seven communities from among the"Sikkimese of Nepali origin" as " socially and educationally backward Classes (OBCs)". Consequently, Bhujel, Gurung, Limbu, Magar, Rai, Sunuwar and Tamang were declared OBC in Sikkim on June2, 1994.

The fourth general election for the state assembly in Sikkim was held on November 16, 1994 and P K Chamling fought it on slogan of "Bhasha *Na: Bhat*"(Language is immaterial for associating; it is the food which, that unites us) on behalf of his political party, Sikkim Democratic Front (SDF) against Bhandari's claim for getting the recognition of Nepali as a national language in India. Electorate rejected the latter and Chamling formed the government with 19 members in the house of 32. By the time fifth general election was declared in 1999, Chamling had consolidated his position by according to recognition to ten ethnic languages (Nepali, Lepcha, Bhutia, Limbu, Magar, Rai, Gurung, Sherpa, Newari and Tamang) as the official languages of the state in 1995; promised to include all sections of Nepalese as the OBCs in 1996; and opposed merger of Sikkim with that of Darjeeling in 1997.

By providing reservations of 12 seats for Bhutia and Lepchas and 1 Sangha seat, it in a way has protected the minority rights and this can be seen in the multiculturalism policy which is encompassive and accommodative of different multi-ethnic groups and is successful in further maintaining peace among the multi-ethnic groups. And the left seat that is 17 seats out of 32 is for general communities. This in a way provides equal distribution of power and equality in representation in politics.

Though the Nepali language is spoken by everyone and the lingua-franca of language is been introduced as a subject in schools and colleges. This in a way creates a sense of belongingness and togetherness. The state is Nepali but still each ethnic group's language can be used for interaction and every ethnic group.

Many of the important festivals of different ethnic groups are recognized as government holidays such as Sakhewa, Saga Dawa, tendong-lho-rum-faat, buddha purnima, dussehra, diwali, losoong, lochaar, Iman Singh Chemjong Diwas etc. all these sorts of inclusive policy of every ethnic communities initiates a great step towards maintaining peace in present day and in future as well.

Also, if we see the role of political parties as an institution right from the period of former first Chief Minister of Sikkim Shri. Kazi Lendup Dorjee Khangsharpa the first political party known as SSC lead by him always focused on maintaining harmony among ethnic communities and promoted secularism and democracy and till today we can find political parties articulating the idea of inclusiveness policy and considers the voice of every ethnic communities. Thus, it can be said that institutions such as political parties also play a significant role in articulating peace among ethnic communities.

The religious, cultural, and intellectual dimension of the Sikkimese society is promoted. In fact, the government has reemphasized on secularism as the core traditional value of Sikkimese society and polity. It has strengthened the tenets of secularism by supporting the setting up of increased number of places of worship belonging to all religions and communities. Sikkim's glorious culture has found expression in its literature, folklore, music, dance, and drama reaching new standards of excellence. This in a way promotes social harmony in the society (Singh 2008, p. 199).

Communities, cultures, religions, and customs of different hues intermingle freely here in Sikkim to constitute a homogenous blend. Hindu temples coexist with Buddhist monasteries and there are even churches, Muslim mosques, and Sikh 'Gurdwaraa'. Although the Buddhists with monasteries all over the state are the most conspicuous religious group, they are in fact a minority constituting only 28 percent of the population. The majority 68 percent profess Hinduism. The predominant communities are the Lepchas, Bhutias and the Nepalis. In the urban areas many plainsmen- Marwaris, Biharis, Bengalis, South Indians, and Punjabis- have also settled and they are mostly engaged in business and government service.

Because of development and construction activities in the state, a small part of the population consists of migrant laborers from the plains and from Nepal: plumbers, masons and carpenters from Orissa, Bihar, and West Bengal. There are also a few Tibetan refugees settled in Sikkim. Cultural and economic forces are reshaping the way of the life of the Sikkimese. Despite the fact of such powerful external influences, Sikkimese has proved to be resilient accepting the benefits of progress while retaining their ethnic identity. (Singh 2008, pp.248-249).

Sikkim as a state is still able to maintain peace through various means. Also, there is never been an issue of territory dispute among the ethnic communities of Sikkim because the idea of Sikkimese identity prevails over it. And further sustains peace.

Conclusion

CONCLUSION

Sikkim, a small Himalayan state of the Indian union, is a multi-cultural society cohabited by a multiple cultural-linguistic group of which the Lepchas (also called Rongs/Monpas), the Bhutias (also called Denzongpas/Lhopas) and the Nepalis (also called Gorkhas/Paharias) forms major communities in Sikkim. Lamaist Buddhism and Hinduism are the two major religions and apart from it we find Christianity also. Besides, a small group of the population still practices animism, found particularly among the Lepchas and mongoloid stocks of the Nepalis. (Gurung 2011)

Over the decade's social mobility among the three ethnic communities has increased along with the events of inter-community marriages and social interaction though maintenance of distinct ethnic identity is maintained.

The Bhutia people, who settled in Sikkim in greater number during the early 17th century, came in conflict with the indigenous Lepcha people. The Bhutias began the process of Tibetanising the Lepchas by converting them to their own religion, by establishing matrimonial relations with them and by destroying the distinct Lepcha culture and tradition. This process of Tibetanisation which ensued in the wake of the Bhutias settlement resulted in some success that culminated in the growth of an upper Lepcha class. But the discord between the two communities could not be removed even with the passage of time. By consecrating a Tibetan king, the Bhutias established rule in Sikkim and gained a favourable position.

The settlement of the Nepalese in Sikkim which started after the conclusion of the treaty between the British governments of India and Sikkim in 1861 and which was proliferated during 1890s incited opposition from the Bhutias people because of the Gurkha invasion in Sikkim in the 18th century who raided different areas of Sikkim and had destroyed monasteries along with the Sikkimese capital of Rabdentse.

The Nepalis in general were not being considered as original inhabitants i.e., Sikkim Subjects. Based on such issue that is Sikkim Subjects, the then society in Sikkim was divided into two main ethnic groups. Besides, a law was in force prohibiting land alienation by hereditary state subjects in favour of non-hereditary subjects. Along with this, the land revenue imposed upon the farmers of these three ethnic groups was exceptionally discriminatory. (Datta 1994, p.75)

After 1947 the political parties like the Sikkim National Party emerged as a pro-Chogyal Bhutias-Lepcha party, Praja Sammelan, Swatantra Dal or Scheduled Caste League etc. And Janata Party of a later period were nothing but the political forum of different groups of Nepali community. Only the Sikkim National Congress which emerged through the merger of several small parties represented all the different communities.

The parity system which was introduced during the first general election in 1953, as a basis for distribution of political, economic, and other facilities among the different communities, was deeply influenced by keeping the Bhutias-Lepcha and Nepali communities disintegrated.

A few systems in the name of protection of the Bhutias-Lepcha interest however, continued to promote discord between the ethnic groups. The land revenue imposed upon the farmers of the three communities, which was in force up to 1966, was highly discriminatory. For the same acres and quality of land the Nepalese had to pay higher tax than the Bhutias-Lepchas.[1]

Considering all the above-mentioned factors it indicates the ethnic conflict which happened before post-merger at the time of monarchic form of government and it even indicates that "after the treaty of 1890, the British govt. openly started to patronise Nepali immigration in Sikkim and the Nepalese, in huge numbers were coming and settling there.

The helpless Bhutias in utter frustration had to reconcile with this. But in different times the conflict between these communities took violent turns leading even to bloodshed." (Sengupta 1985, p.19)

This shows that there was ethnic violence in Sikkim, and the ethnic violence can be seen in the form of protest monarchical form of government which always initiated policies which created an alienation feeling among the ethnic groups of Sikkim. It is always the (state/ govt./institutions/political parties) that ensures peace and harmony among ethnic groups. For instance, if we take the case of the emergence of Sikkimese identity which came into existence in broader context particularly after the durbar[2] recognised the earliest settlers as legal settlers who had been given the status of Sikkimese. They are referred to as Sikkimese by Sikkim subject Regulations, 1961 (Rao 1978: 20-21) cited in (Datta 1994, p.77).

The main intention of this recognition was to enhance the level of economic and political interests of the ruling elites by monopolizing their dominance over the limited resources. It excluded Nepalis who formed 70% of the population in Sikkim. To elucidate the role of the state it is the state itself which ensures conflict and on the other hand it is the state only which promotes peace such as on the similar issue of Sikkim subject Regulation where Nepali community was alienated and created a hatred feeling and at the same could sustain peace among ethnic communities by formulating policies which later, to allay the fears of the Nepalese all reference to the communities was deleted from the regulations with effect from 16th January, 1962.

Even in the 20th century we can see that the oppressed of Sikkim who was under monarchic form of government where a party of different organizations was clubbed and Sikkim State Congress was formed and put their demands to ruler (a) abolition of landlordism, which was a serious issue for generating ethnic conflict. (b) Formation of an interim government and (c) accession of Sikkim to India.

The State Congress leaders met the ruler on 9th December 1947 with their above charter of demands. (Sinha 1975, p.285) Now drawing this issue it is clearly sensible that state was creating problem among ethnic groups as the politics of Sikkim is always based on ethnic communities. Which is cited as, *"But in different times the conflict between these communities took violent turns leading even to bloodshed."* (Sengupta 1985, p.19). Again, the Maharaja was advised to go with the changing time and pay heed towards the demand of the common man. Some land reforms were made immediately such as abolition of lessee system, end of various forms of unpaid labours, restructuring of judicial system. These changes could to some extent maintain peace, but the end of monarchy was sure to happen.

At the end of the monarchy the Govt. of India took a clear stand on democratic principles.

The famous tripartite agreement[3] of 1974 envisaged ruler to be a constitutional head,[4] establishment of a responsible government with democratic rights, rule of law, fundamental rights, independent judiciary, adult franchise, and executive and legislative powers to the peoples' representatives. Article 5 of the agreement envisages: "the system of election shall be so organised as to make the (state) Assembly adequately representative of the various section of the population. The size and composition of the assembly and of the executive council shall be such as maybe prescribed from time to time, care being taken to ensure that no single section of the population acquires a dominating position due mainly to its *ethnic origin*, and that the rights and interests of the Sikkimese Bhutias-Lepcha origin and of Sikkimese Nepali, which includes Tsongs and Scheduled castes origin, are fully protected". (Sinha 1975, p.289). This sort of policy formulation clearly shows how a state is efficient enough in ensuring the protection and stabilising the growing issues or conflicts among the ethnic communities.

After the post-merger of Sikkim with the Indian union in 1975, we can see many changes and with the opting of democracy, it in a way was a first step towards ensuring ethnic harmony between communities because democracy provides a space for belongingness and togetherness and acceptance which is promoted by the idea of secularism which is there in the constitution of India and is well practiced by the state Sikkim. To illustrate one example of state that takes a step to ensure peace is through the "Article 371 F (g) of the constitution which provides that " the Governor of Sikkim shall have special responsibility for peace and for an equitable arrangement for ensuring the social and economic advancement of different sections of the population of Sikkim and in the discharge of his special responsibility under this clause the Governor of Sikkim shall, subject to such directions as the president may, from time to time, deem fit to issue, act in his discretion". (Sengupta 1985, p.237)

Such practices and clause itself play a huge role in ensuring peace and equality among the communities of Sikkim and assuaging the disparities among ethnic communities. The role of Governor also indicates the responsibility towards sustaining peace. Sikkim was merged with India in 1975 and introduction of parliamentary democracy generated expectation that ethnic discrimination and politics based on ethno-cultural identity would slowly make a path for equitable and secular political mobilization. But the Government of India decided to continue with the provisions which existed in Sikkim in pre-merger times. To say in other words, the state rules which discriminated the Nepalis on ethnic grounds such as Revenue Order No.1, settlement laws, communal voting, and representation system etc., were provided constitutional sanctions (Article 371 F) under the parliamentary-democratic and secular constitution of India. This also shows how the Govt. policies can contribute to the ethnic disparities. It is definite that state ensures peace but on the other hand even such policies can accentuate the division among ethnic communities, one example to understand this is, the central government had asked the state government to recommend names of communities for the representation of Scheduled Tribes list for Sikkim as early as 1976.

But, contrary to the desire of the central government to include various tribal groups of Sikkim namely Bhutias, Lepcha, Limboo, Tamang, Gurung, Mangar, Rai etc., in the tribal list, the state government recommended for inclusion of only the Lepchas and Bhutias. The policy of the state government denying scheduled tribes' status to some deserving communities in favour of certain other groups created alienation and discrimination among the groups who were denied Scheduled Tribes status. (Gurung 2011, pp.413-414). This in a way can germinate the seeds towards ethnic conflict and for this type of situation the state has a vital role in maintaining less intensity of conflict. The state however can rectify the inadequacy or deficiency. As such politics can be used not only to confirm group status but to enhance it also. (in 1985, Mr. Bhandari demanded recognition of the Nepali language in the eight schedules of the Indian constitution. In 1994-95, Mr. Chamling demanded the same status for the Bhutias, Lepcha, and Limboo languages).

Therefore, it is the way the government looks at the issue and formulates policy often stir up community resentments and precipitate ethnic consciousness. (Sinha 1975, p.416)

The election campaigns of Sikkim Congress and the Sikkim Gorkha Prajatantrik Party favouring the interests of the concerned community also contributed towards the intensification of ethnic tensions. But Sikkim Sangram Parishad's call for Sikkimese Identity transcending Nepali, Bhutias and Lepcha identity has helped in plummeting ethnic conflict. In contrast, the ruling SDF party, even though had clear ethnic bias in the beginning, has been, to a hefty extent, doing well in mollifying ethnic conflict/ tension through carefully orchestrated policies of accommodation of ascriptive interest with that of economic sumptuousness. This makes clear and substantiates the fact that the **State** can spawn a particular type of perception which may possibly either control or heighten ethnic conflict.

But with the course of time, there is a varying dynamic with the demands of the ethnic communities of Sikkim. For instance, the issues like the bulk of Lepchas feel that the Bhutias have deprived of them the distinct position in the society and cornered the benefits supposed for them as scheduled tribes. They want protection of their land from the Bhutias and equal representation with that of the Bhutias in all respects. The Lepchas are separate community and want to be acknowledged as Lepchas and positively not as B-L. (Sinha 1975, P.419). The reservation of seats in the political institutions and recognition of certain old laws of Sikkim after the merger are viewed as a distinct political/legal identity of the people of Sikkim. But the rebuff of the political/legal identity[5] for the Nepalis and prolongation of old Sikkimese laws which discriminated the Nepalis in the past constitutes major concern and apprehension for the Sikkimese Nepalis. Along with this the influx from other parts of India has further aroused the unease for Sikkimese people. Thus, every bit of these areas must be looked upon cautiously and handled to ensure ethnic harmony among the various communities.

[1] Sengupta, Nirmalananda. *State Government and Politics: Sikkim.* Sterling Publishing Pvt. Ltd, New Delhi, 1985.

[2] During the time of Chogyal.

[3] After the abolishment of Chogyal, the provisions of the indo-Sikkim treaty, Tripartite Agreement, and the Govt. of the Indian ACT, 1974 were made inoperative. See (Sinha 1975).

[4] Ruler (Chogyal) to be a constitutional head, was later removed, while merging Sikkim with India, the state assembly met in an emergency season and passed this resolution: saying "The institution of Chogyal (the head of

the state) is hereby abolished And Sikkim shall henceforth be a constituent unit of India". See (Sinha 1975, p.290)

[5] Abolition of Nepali seats in 1979/80.

Reference

REFERENCE :

Arora, Vibha. "Roots and the Route of Secularism in Sikkim." *Economic and Political Weekly,* 2006:9.

Basnet, L.B (1974). *Sikkim: A Short Political History.* New Delhi: S Chand and Company.

Baumann, Timothy. "Defining Ethnicity." *The SAA Achaeological record.,* 2004:3.

Badan, B.S., and Bhatt, Harish. (2007), Culture and Tourism, Commonwealth, New Delhi.

Bareh, H.M. (2001). Encyclopedia of North-East India: Sikkim. New Delhi: Mittal Publication; Volume VII. ISBN-81-7099-794-1. 25.p.

Bhattachryya, Kumar Pranab. (1984), Aspects of Cultural History of Sikkim, K.P.Bagchi and Company, Calcutta.

Birundha, Dhulasi, V. (2003), Environmental Challenges Towards Tourism, Kanishka Publishers, Distributors, New Delhi.

Bhadra, Madhumita (1992). *Sikkim: Democracy and Social Change.* Minerma Associates pvt. Ltd.

Bhasin Veena. "Ethnic Relations Among the People of Sikkim." *J. Soc. Sci.,* 2002:20.

Burkart, AJ. & Medilk, S. (1981). Tourism: Past and Present. London: Heinemann.

Butler, R. (1999). Tourism: An evolutionary perspective.

Barman, Arup, and Singh, Ranjit and Rao, Y. Venkata. (2010). Empowering Tribes Through Cultural Tourism in India – A Dream Project on ICT Integration (November 30, 2010).

Biju Kumar, V. (2000): In Response to Development Crisis: Decentralized Planning and Development in Kerala, Journal of Rural Development, NIRD, Hyderabad, 19(3), pp. 339-369

Chakrabarti, Anjan., (2009), Economic Development and Employment in Sikkim, Authorspress, New Delhi.

Chakraborty, Jyotirmoy. "Sikkim Elections and Casteist Politics." *Economic and Political Weekly,* 2000: 3805-3807.

Chatterji, S.K. (1974). Kirata-Jana-Krti: the Indo-Mongoloids, their Contribution to the History and Culture of India, The Asiatic Society, Calcutta.

Choedon, Dr. Yeshe. "Cultural Evolution of Sikkim: A Survey. "*Bulletin of Tibetology* 73-76.

Choudhury, M. (1997). Development Project Vis-à-vis Ethno-Religious Sentiments: The Rathong Chu Imbroglio in Sikkim, Occasional paper No.12, Centre for

Chamling, Pawan. (2002), Speeches on the ocassiom of 50th National Development Meeting on 32st December, New Delhi.

Das, Dinesh (2013). 'Tourism Industry in North-East Indian States: Prospect and Problems'. *Journal of Global Research Methodology* , 2(7), 1-6.

Dewan, Dr. Dick B. *Education in Sikkim An Historical Retrospect Pre-Merger and Post-Merger Period.* Tender Buds Academy, July 2012.

Dhamala, R.R. (1994): 'Panchayati Raj Institution in Sikkim: Participation and Development', in Sikkim: Society, Polity, Economy, Environment, ed. by M.P. Lama, Indus, New Delhi, p. 64.

Development of the Himalayas', in Development of Hill Areas: Issues and Approaches, ed. by T.S. Papola et al, Himalaya Publishing House, Bombay, p. 413.

Draft Ninth Plan of Sikkim, 1997-2002, Bureau of Economics and Statistics, Government of Sikkim, 1998, pp. 269-270.

Foning, A.R. (1987). Lepcha, My Vanishing Tribe, Sterling, New Delhi.

Gorer, G. (1938). Himalayan Village: An Account of the Lepchas of Sikkim, Reprinted 1987. Gian Publishing House, Delhi.

Geertz, C. (1973). *The Intrepretation of Culture: Selected Essay.* New York: Inc Publisher.

Gurung, Suresh Kumar (2011). *Sikkim Ethnicity and Political Dynamics A Triadic Prespective.*New Delhi: Kunal Books.

Government of India (2008) Sikkim Development Report, Planning Commission, New Delhi.

Government of Sikkim (2010), Sikkim Tourism Polocy 2010, Tourism Department, Gangtok.

Government Reports Anonymous, Primary Census Abstract, Census of India, Sikkim, 2001. (2001). Directorate of Census Operations, Govt. of India.

Gowloog, R.R. (1995). Lingthem Revisited: Social Change in A Lepcha Village in North Sikkim, Har Anand Publishers, New Delhi.

Garrod, B. and Fyall, A. (2001). Heritage Tourism: A question of definitions. Annals of tourism research, 28(4), 1049-1052.

Gee, C.Y.' and Fyaos-Sola, E. (1997). International Tourism: A global perspective. Madrid: World Tourism Organisation.

Giri, Mukund. "Sikkim: Politics of Inclusiveness and One-Party Dominance." *Economic and Political Weekly,* 2009:3.

Gupta, Ranjan. "Sikkim: The Merger with India." *Asian Survey* (University of California Press) 15 (September 1975): 786-798.

Hall, C., and Page Stephen, (2001), Tourism in South and South east Asia, Butterworth-Heniemann, Oxford.

Hofstede, G. (1997). Cultures and Organizations: Software of the mind. New York: McGraw Hill; 1 edition. ISBN-10: 0070293074 | ISBN-13: 978-0070293076. 279 p.

Herskovits, M. J (1948). *Man and his Works: The Science of Cultural Anthropology.* New York: knopf publisher.

Ismayilov, Gursel G. "Ethnic Conflicts and their Causes." 17.

Jacob E.Safra & Jorge Aguilar-Cauz (2013). *Britannica Reference Encyclopedia.* London: Encyclopedia Britannica, Inc.

Jervis, N (2006). What is culture? New York.

Joshi, H.G (2004). *Sikkim Past and Present.* New Dehli: Krishna Mittal.

Kamra, K.K (2009). *Basic of Tourism: Theory, Operation and Practice.* New Delhi: Kanishka Publisher.

Kazi, J N. *Against the Tide.* Gangtok: Hill Media Publication, 1994.

Lama, Mahendra P, ed. *Sikkim Society Polity Economy Environment.* New Delhi: Indus Publishing Company, 1994.

Mahajan, Gurpreet. "Responding to Identity Conflicts: Multiculturalism and the Pursuit of Peaceful Co-Existence." *South Asian Journal of Peacebuilding* 2 (2010): 10.

Mead, M (1953). *The Study of Culture at Distance.* Chicago: Chicago Press.

Malinowski, B (1931). 'Culture: In The Era Seligman'. *Encyclopedia of Social Sciences,* 4, 621-646.

Minkov, M (2013). *Cross Cultural Analysis: The Science and Art of Comparing the World's Modern Socities and theit*

Cultures. United Kingdom: Sage publications.

Moktan, R (2013). *Sikkim: Darjeeling: Compendium of Documents.* R.Moktan: Kalimpong.

Nye, J (2009). *Understanding International Conflict.* New York: Pearson.

Padhi, M. M (2014). 'Emergence of Tourism in the Sustainable Growth Of India: An Empirical Analysis'. *National Monthly Refereed Journal Of Reserch In Commerce and Managment , 1* (8), 161-167.

Phadnis, Urmila. "Ethnic Dimensions of Sikkimese Politics: The 1979 Elections." *Asian Survey* (University of California Press) 20 (1980): 1236-1252.

Rai, Dhanraj. "Monarchy and Democracy in Sikkim and the Contribution of Kazi Lhendup Dorjee Khangsherpa." *International Journal of Scientific and Research Publications* 3, no. 9 (September 2014): 13.

Rudolph, Jr. Joseph R., ed. *Encyclopedia of Modern Ethnic Conflict.* Greenwood Press Westport, Conneticut, 2003.

R. P. R (2014). 'Emerging Environmental Issues With The Development Of Tourism Industry In India': A Study. *International Journal of Development Research , 4* (5), 995-999.

Sharma, Tika Prasad (2008). 'Traditional Handloom and Handicrafts of Sikkim'. *Indian Journal of Traditional Knowledge,* 9(2): 375-377.

Sengupta, Nirmalananda (1985). *State Government and Politics: Sikkim.* New Delhi: Sterling Publisher Pvt. Ltd.

Singh, R.S. Arha and Latika (2008). *Glimpses of Sikkim.* Jaipur: Abd Publisher.

Sinha, AC (1975). *Politics of Sikkim: A Sociological Study.* Faridabad: Thompson Press.

Sinha, AC, "Resource Distribution and Multiple Ethnic Identity of Sikkim." In Asian Highland Societies: *In Anthropological Perspective,* edited by Christoph Furer von

Haimendorf. New Delhi: Sterling Publishing Pvt. Ltd, 1981.

Sinha, A.C. "Search for Kirat Identity Trends of De-Sanskritization among the Nepamul Sikkimese." *Peace and Democracy in South Asia*, 2006: 22.

Sinha, AC. "The Politics of Identity Formation in Sikkim." *Dialogue (A Quarterly Journal of Astha Bharati)*, 2009.

Subba, TB and AC. Sinha, *Nepalis in Northeast India: A Community in search of an identity.* New Delhi: Indus Publishing Company, 2003.

Subba, TB. *Politics of Culture: A study of Three Kirat Communities in the Eastern Himalayas.* Hyderabad: Orient Longman, 1999.

Shrestha, B. G (2015). *The Newars Of Sikkim: ReinventingLanguage, Culture, and Identity in the Diaspora.* Nepal: Viraj Books.

Subba, G. M. (2013). 'Fluid Boundaries and Fluid Identities- The Study Of Limboo Tribe Of Sikkim'. *Journal Of Humanities and Social Science , 15* (2), 56-63.

Subba, J.R. (2008). 'Indeginous Knowledge on bio-resources management for livelihood of thr people'. *Indian Journal of Traditional Knowledge, 8(1),55-64.*

Tong, Rebecca. "Explaining Ethnic Peace: The Importance of Institutions." *Res Publica-Journal of Undergraduate Research,* 2009:16.

Tran, Hong. *Chogyal's Sikkim: Tax, Land & Clan Politics.* 10-1-2012.

Thapa, J. P. (2014). 'Some Nonfermented Ethnic Foods of Sikkim in India'. *Journal of Ethnic Foods , 29-33.*

Triandis, A. P. (1987). 'On the Universality of Social Psychology'. *Journal of Cross-Cultural Psychology , 18* (4), 471-498. Theobald, Global Tourism. Wobum: Butterworth-Heinemann.

Vaiphei, Lianboi. "Addressing Multiculturalism for Ethnic Equations in Manipur." *Eastern Quarterly*, March 2008: 229-237.

https://documents.saa.org/container/docs/default-source/doc-publications/publications/the-saa-archaeological-record/tsar-2004/sep04.pdf?sfvrsn=6a0432b6_2#page=14

Berreman, Gerald D. 1972 Race, Cast, and Other Invidious Distinctions in Social Stratifi- cation. *Race* 13:385–414.

Cohen, Abner. 1974 Introduction: The Lesson of Ethnicity. In *Urban Ethnicity*, edit- ed by A. Cohen, pp. Ix–xxiv. Tavistock Publications, London.

Jones, Sian. 1997 *The Archaeology of Ethnicity: Constructing Identities in the Past and Present*. Routledge Press, London, and New York.